MORE
FROM THE QUARRIES
OF
LAST CHANCE GULCH

JON AXLINE
ELLEN BAUMLER
CHERE JIUSTO
LEANNE KURTZ
HARRIETT C. MELOY
RICHARD B. ROEDER
DAVE WALTER

HELENA
INDEPENDENT RECORD
Bruce Whittenberg, Publisher

ISBN 1-56037-088-2

Prepared for publication by
American & World Geographic Publishing

CONTENTS

BUILDINGS

EVENTS

INTRODUCTION

꧁꧂

In 1951 the lifelong Helena newspaperman William C. Campbell published *From the Quarries of Last Chance Gulch: A "News-History" of Helena*. Although this volume covers only the years from 1864 to 1889, it represents the first concerted attempt to tell the story of the Helena community.

Campbell's work proved so well-received that—to mark the Territorial Centennial and the 100th anniversary of Helena's founding—he released a companion volume in 1964. The second volume of *From the Quarries of Last Chance Gulch* extends the newspaper-excerpt history to 1900, and it too gained statewide acclaim. When Campbell died in 1989, his longtime employer, the (Helena) *Independent Record,* justifiably noted that his *Quarries* books capped a remarkable journalistic career.

In late March 1994, the *Independent Record*'s Associate Editor, Dave Shors, unveiled the first installment of a weekly local-history series in Campbell's old paper. In the initial piece, Jon Axline observed:

> A team of Helena historians has assembled to research and write of places, events, and people that have made Helena what it is today. Some of the stories will be amusing and others sad; the majority will fall somewhere in-between. In the process, we hope to set the record straight on what happened in the "Queen City of the Rockies" and to its people, giving our readers a feeling for what it was like to live here from the early 1860s until the present.

Columnists agreed upon the column's title—"More From Quarries from Last Chance Gulch"—primarily to recognize William C. Campbell for his pioneering efforts to tell the Helena story.

Seven core columnists wrote in regular rotation: Jon Axline, Ellen Baumler, Chere Jiusto, Leanne Kurtz, Harriett C. Meloy,

Richard B. Roeder, and Dave Walter. From time to time, several guest writers addressed local-history topics that ranged from Vivian Paladin's pieces on the contested location of the "Four Georgians'" gold discovery to Kim Morrison's columns on the Van Orsdel site in the valley to Pat Bik's depiction of Helena's Chinese community.

The variety that Axline promised did, indeed, develop through the year. "More From the Quarries" stretched from such specific sites as Mount Helena Park, Central School, and the West Main Street lime kilns to such community events as the 1894 "Capital Election" celebration to such prominent, diverse Helenans as Cornelius Hedges, John Neill, "Chicago Joe," and Belle Winestine. Without fail, the soundly-researched columns alerted, entertained, and educated. On occasion—by addressing such topics as urban renewal, prostitution, and the location of Helena's first gold discovery—they provoked controversy.

One of the advantages of working in Montana's recorded past is that the time period is manageable. The "Four Georgians" discovered gold along Last Chance Creek 131 years ago—less than two full lifetimes. "More From the Quarries" columnists can trace their telling of the Helena story directly to that 1864 beginning, through the first volume of William Campbell's *From the Quarries of Last Chance Gulch*. Norman B. Holter—who was born in Helena in 1868 and grew up with the people who founded the community—penned the introduction to that 1951 work. The ties of every current Helenan to his past remain exceedingly close, and strong.

A weekly look at that past provides several benefits to Helenans. Well-researched, well-written local history captures the special rhythms and themes of a city. By delving into the community's common past—a past that plays out against readers' most familiar historical setting—local history can sharpen Helenans' focus on their shared heritage. It can emphasize our cultural similarities, rather than our immediate differences. Further, it can build a solid appreciation for the cityscape.

Accurate local history is "history that matters" because it tells the real story. By isolating and describing a wide range of specific sites, specific events, and specific people, local history moves beyond the community's hackneyed, oft-repeated tales. It corrects the myths; it explains the complexity of circumstances. Without exception, the truth about a community's past is more compelling than any of the fictionalized, embellished accounts. Helena offers its citizens a truly rich story, and those citizens have long appreciated the importance of that story.

From the beginning, the "More From the Quarries from Last Chance Gulch" articles have tried to develop among readers a sense of the distinction of the Helena place. That place is basic to our common cultural past, our "group memory," our shared heritage. The common bond among "More From the Quarries" columnists is the hope that their efforts will enhance a sense of the city's past. For, knowing the particulars of that past will help us to deal with problems when they develop in our common future in this place.

In the largest sense, a collection of pieces about Helena's past emphasizes the lessons of historical change and continuity. Helenans who develop an appreciation for the city's historical context gain a strong "sense of place." That advantage becomes particularly useful when local controversies pit the preservation/reuse of "the old" against the headlong rush into "the new," simply for the sake of "newness."

Many a Western local-historian talks of the "warp and woof" of his community's past, but he often is left to deal with a threadbare carpet. "More From the Quarries" writers, on the other hand, work constantly with the "deep pile" of Helena's history. No doubt about it, lots of things really happened right here!

Some of this richness derives from Helena's selection in 1874 as Montana's capital. Much more of it can be attributed to the diversity of Helena's story—and particularly to the varied origins of her citizens. Fortunately, Helenans always have recognized this richness. If you are a local-history aficionado, Helena is the place to be a rug salesman.

With sincere gratitude the writers acknowledge the immense support and unfailing cooperation of the *Independent Record*'s Associate Editor, Dave Shors, in producing both the weekly column and this volume. Dave's editorial abilities are exceeded only by his personal thoughtfulness and sincerity.

Barbara Fifer, Brad Hurd, and Teresa Record of American & World Geographic Publishing, have imposed a thoughtful, effective order upon an assortment of writing styles and selections. We are grateful for their experience, understanding, and advice. In addition, the entire writing corps owes a special thanks to Ellen Baumler for her organizational abilities. Without Ellen's gentle reminders, sensitive handling of disparate personalities, and skillful work as an intermediary, the "More From the Quarries" column never would have matured.

Finally, to the readers of the weekly "More From the Quarries" column, we extend our gratitude for your continued interest, suggestions, and encouragement. Helenans hold a rich heritage in common, and this volume only begins to document the wealth of that heritage. The excavation of Helena's history will continue.

Richard B. Roeder
Dave Walter
Helena, Montana
May, 1995

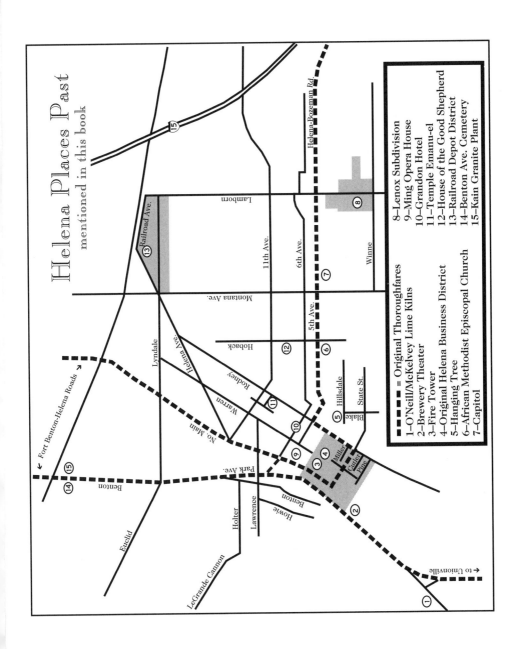

Helena Places Past
mentioned in this book

- = Original Thoroughfares
1–O'Neill/McKelvey Lime Kilns
2–Brewery Theater
3–Fire Tower
4–Original Helena Business District
5–Hanging Tree
6–African Methodist Episcopal Church
7–Capitol
8–Lenox Subdivision
9–Ming Opera House
10–Grandon Hotel
11–Temple Emanu-el
12–House of the Good Shepherd
13–Railroad Depot District
14–Benton Ave. Cemetery
15–Kain Granite Plant

Fort Benton-Helena Roads
to Unionville →
Helena-Bozeman Rd.
Railroad Ave.
Montana Ave.
11th Ave.
6th Ave.
5th Ave.
Lamborn
Winne
Hoback
Hillsdale
State St.
Blake
Miller
Cutler
Pine
Park Ave.
Benton
Howie
Lawrence
Holter
LeGrande Cannon
Euclid
Benton
Lyndale
Helena Ave.
Rodney
Warren
No. Main

PEOPLE

Vigilante "Justice"

❧

BY JON AXLINE

[James] Daniels was indicted for a crime he did not commit. He was tried by a court without jurisdiction. He was sentenced by a judge without authority. He was reprieved by a governor by mistake, and he was hung by the mob.

Nathaniel P. Langford

Perhaps one of the most infamous photographs of early Helena is the image of Jim Daniels dangling from the hanging tree once located near the intersection of Hillsdale and Blake streets. While the gruesome photograph may be well known, the events leading up to the hanging and its role in the political battle then raging in Montana Territory is obscure.

According to Nathaniel Langford, Jim Daniels had already murdered a man in California before coming to Helena in 1865. Langford described Daniels as "hardened to vice and crime, and, possibly, was one of the worst of all ruffians..." Basically a classic example of a frontier ne'er-do-well, Daniels spent his days in the mining camp drinking and playing cards.

On November 29, 1865, Daniels was playing poker with Andrew Gartley in Con Price's Belmont Saloon on Main Street. Apparently, Daniels caught Gartley cheating and a scuffle broke out. Gartley pushed Daniels against a stove and pulled a revolver. Daniels responded by stabbing Gartley twice with a large knife.

Mortally wounded, Gartley died the following day. The *Montana Post* lamented this as "Another terrible warning to young men against the temptations of the bar and gaming table."

The Helena vigilantes immediately seized Daniels and turned him over to Deputy Neil Howie. Newly appointed District Court Judge Lyman E. Munson presided over the trial.

For some unknown reason, Munson charged Daniels under the laws of Nebraska Territory rather than under Montana statutes. After a short trial held in Virginia City, Daniels was convicted of m a n s l a u g h t e r, received a three-year sentence and was ordered to pay a $1,000 fine. He was incarcerated in the Virginia City jail.

Daniels was hanged on March 2, 1866.

Many Helena citizens, however, believed Daniels' sentence too harsh and petitioned acting Governor Thomas Francis Meagher for a reprieve. They asserted, and Meagher agreed, that Daniels had acted in self-defense when he killed Gartley.

Meagher, "while under the influence of an unfortunate habit," granted Daniels a reprieve on February 22, 1866. He was released from jail after serving only three weeks of his sentence.

Meagher either did not understand his legal authority or chose to ignore the law when he granted Daniels a pardon. Under the terms of the act that created Montana Territory, the governor had only the power to grant a stay of execution to prisoners convicted of capital crimes. The authority to grant reprieves or pardons rested solely with the president of the United States.

When Thomas Francis Meagher disappeared in July 1867, many believed the vigilantes, irate over the mishandling of the Daniels affair, were responsible.

Daniels was not convicted of first degree murder and, therefore, did not qualify for a reprieve or pardon.

An enraged Judge Munson wrote to Meagher on March 1 demanding that he revoke the order and return Daniels to prison. When Meagher declined, Munson ordered the U.S. Marshall to re-arrest Daniels. Unfortunately, by that time, Daniels was on his way back to Helena.

Vowing to get even with those who testified against him, Daniels arrived back in Helena at about 9 P.M. on March 2, 1866.

The vigilantes immediately surrounded him and he was hanged within the hour; Meagher's reprieve was still in his pocket.

The mob attached a note to the back of Daniels' coat threatening Meagher with a similar fate if he continued to grant clemency to miscreants. Daniels' body remained suspended from the tree until the next day when he was buried in the vicinity of Central School. In 1933 city construction crews unearthed the body and placed the bones on display.

The vigilantes hanged Daniels as a lesson to Thomas Meagher and not because he'd done anything wrong. While Langford believed Daniels deserved death, he felt the vigilantes had no right to inflict it and that they had "exceeded the boundaries of right and justice and became themselves the violators of law and propriety."

The incident proved to be the one of the last straws in the territory's tolerance of the politically erratic Meagher. Just three days after Daniels' death, Meagher convened the legislature to help put the territory's affairs in order. A Democrat, Meagher vacillated between the Democratic majority in the state and the ultra-conservative Republican party headed by Lyman Munson, the judge in the Jim Daniels case.

Republicans objected to the political edge enjoyed by the Democrats in the legislature and vehemently opposed it (eventually all the laws enacted by the 1866 legislature were declared null and void).

When Meagher disappeared in July 1867, many believed the vigilantes, irate over the mishandling of the Daniels affair, were responsible. Although a scoundrel, Jim Daniels unwittingly became a pawn in the partisan power struggle raging between the Republicans and Democrats in Montana after the Civil War.

The hanging was not officially sanctioned by the Executive Committee of the Vigilante organization, but, still, Daniels' death was a skirmish in that struggle.

As for the hanging tree, it hosted several other "necktie parties" until April 1870 when the last execution was held under its branches. In 1875, a Methodist minister cut the tree down with the excuse that recent floods had undermined its roots, making it a hazard to his barn. With its removal, a grim chapter in early Helena's judicial history ended.

UP IN THE SKY

❧❧❧

BY LEANNE KURTZ

Every day like clockwork, big Delta airships ferry hundreds of passengers in and out of Helena, while dozens of smaller private planes and charters dot the sky. These days, we take for granted our ability to hop on a giant, heavy metal cylinder, climb 40,000 feet into the air at hundreds of miles an hour, dine on some chicken entree while watching a feature film, and reach our desired destination in less than a day. Despite the fact that early Helena pilots had to share runway space with golfers at the Helena Municipal Golf Course (now Bill Roberts Golf Course), and land at the county Fairgrounds for exhibitions, Helena's skies were graced by some of the most famous aviators in the country—among them Cromwell Dixon, Charles Lindbergh and Amelia Earhart.

Helenans craning their necks to watch daredevil pilot Cromwell Dixon attempt to cross the Continental Divide on a September day in 1911 had never heard of frequent flier miles, bright little bags of salty peanuts, or cabin pressure. The only thing on the minds of spectators that day was "Is he gonna make it or not?" Most thought not. Cromwell Dixon was only 19 years old when he arrived in Helena to thrill Montana State Fair-goers in his endeavor to be the first person to fly across the Continental Divide. For a $10,000 purse, Dixon was to wing from the Helena Fairgrounds, over the Rocky Mountains to Blossburg, some eighteen miles west of town. The September 30, 1911 edition of the *Montana Daily Record* recounts the preparations made before Dixon's craft left the ground: "An automobile was sent over to Blossburg ahead of the scheduled time with a mechanician and a can of gasoline. The big bonfire at the top of the main range was kindled and word was sent to Austin and Blossburg." After his Curtiss Biplane with a 60-

horsepower motor reached an elevation of 7,000 feet, Dixon flew from landmark to landmark to navigate his way. Dixon spotted the bonfire (his homing beacon) built by the citizens of Blossburg and landed twenty minutes after leaving the Fairgrounds. He piloted his "flying motor kite" back to Helena without incident and landed himself in the record books. The next day's *Daily Record* read, "It was one of the most dangerous feats ever attempted by man. Death was pitted against daring and daring won. Treacherous winds above, jagged peaks and declivitous slopes below. It was a gamble. Had for one instant fear crept into the heart of the bird-boy...the wind and the rocks would have claimed another victim."

The next day, a triumphant Dixon left Helena for Spokane, where he hoped to again wow the crowd with his mastery of the skies. On the first flight of the day October 2, 1911, Dixon had trouble gaining altitude, was caught by a sudden wind gust and fell 100 feet to the ground. He died 45 minutes later. In 1936, in honor of Dixon's successful feat in Helena, the Forest Service designated the new campground on top of MacDonald Pass "Cromwell Dixon Campground," a name the area retains today.

Sixteen years after Dixon's flight, on September 6, 1927, the dashing Colonel Charles Lindbergh, fresh from his unprecedented solo voyage across the Atlantic, set down the *Spirit of St. Louis* on Helena's Municipal Golf Course. "Women and tots faint," declared the *Montana Record Herald*, describing the scene as thousands of state fair-goers jammed the Fairgrounds waiting for the 25-year-old "tousle-headed boy" to arrive. After appearing to an estimated twenty thousand spectators over the North Hills shortly after 2:00 P.M., Lindbergh executed a textbook landing and was greeted by the "lusty yells of the crowd as it broke through the fence to surround the plane." Governor John Erickson and a party of dignitaries escorted Lindbergh to the Fairgrounds grandstand where he spoke for seven minutes on the future of commercial aviation. "Lindy" was then taken to the Placer Hotel to rest before attending a banquet held in his honor. The next day, Lindbergh left for a short vacation northwest of Helena at Elbow Lake, which was later renamed Lindbergh Lake in honor of his visit.

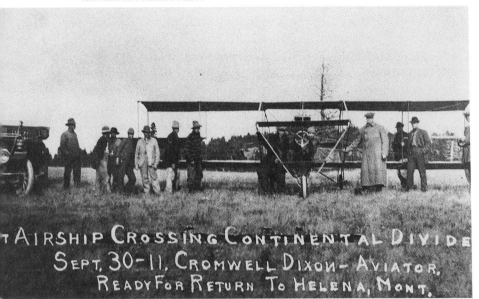

AIRSHIP CROSSING CONTINENTAL DIVIDE
SEPT. 30-11. CROMWELL DIXON — AVIATOR,
READY FOR RETURN TO HELENA, MONT.

It was enough of a thrill for Helenans to host the likes of Dixon and Lindbergh, but residents were again fortunate on January 29, 1933, to receive yet another renowned pilot. Amelia Earhart Putnam visited Helena as part of a Northwest Airways study of a proposed route across the northern United States. At the time, Earhart had already been the first woman to fly solo across the Atlantic (May 1932) and had set cross-country speed records. The airport had since moved east of town near its present location, and upon her arrival, Earhart spoke to a crowd from the second story of the airport administration building. Later that evening, the Placer Hotel hosted a banquet for the celebrated aviatrix where she enraptured the crowd with stories of her "hop" across the "big pond." When Governor Erickson introduced her at the banquet, Earhart joked that since her solo flight across the Atlantic, she had been referred to as "the woman who swam the English Channel," "the woman who swam the Atlantic," and as "Colonel Lindbergh's mother." Earhart recounted the story of her trans-Atlantic flight in

For a $10,000 purse, Cromwell Dixon was to wing from the Helena Fairgrounds, over the Rocky Mountains to Blossburg.

detail, delighting the audience at the Placer. The next day, she addressed an informal joint session of the legislature, encouraging members to participate in aviation and complimenting Helenans on their air facilities. Earhart set many more records in the years following her Helena visit. In June of 1937, she began her infamous aerial expedition around the world and mysteriously disappeared a month later.

Dixon, Lindbergh and Earhart, although among the most illustrious of the aviators to have thrilled Helenans in the last century, are certainly not the only individuals who have dared to defy gravity and leave solid footing behind them. In the days when aviation was still in its infancy, hundreds of daring Montanans crisscrossed the skies, paving the way, so to speak, for the giant metal airships of today to carry the less adventurous among us all over the world.

A Sprig of
Green

BY ELLEN BAUMLER

*I always thought it would be a wonderful thing to be a
tree, so I wear branches in my hair, so I look like one.
For I think it's the branching out, getting the most out
of, and giving the most to life that is the important
idea.*

Belle Fligelman Winestine to Susan Leaphart in
"A Tribute to a Writer," *Independent Record,*
May 5, 1985

Montana women won the right to vote on November 3, 1914.
Men voted to approve the state's suffrage amendment 41,302
to 37,588, but its passage came about because of the hard work
of enthusiastic women supporters. Prominent among these pioneers was Helena's Belle Fligelman Winestine, a diminutive
lady who championed women's rights for most of her ninety-
four years.

Belle, born in 1891, grew up in Helena where her father,
Herman Fligelman, was a partner in the successful New York
Dry Goods Store. Herman, a staunch advocate of education,
sent Belle and her older sister, Frieda, to the University of Wis-
consin at a time when few women went to college. The University at Madison was then an intellectual center for Progressive
reform. Frieda became involved in the suffrage movement, and
Belle, elected president of women students, followed.

Belle returned to Helena in 1914 with a degree in philoso-
phy, just as Montana's suffrage campaign was beginning. She
landed a job with the *Helena Independent,* the paper's first
woman reporter. (In retrospect, Belle wondered if she got the

Norman and Belle Winestine return from Italy on the SS Roma *in 1928.*

job for her writing abilities or because her father's store was a major advertiser.)

As a cub reporter covering a convention of the Montana Federation of Women's Clubs in Lewistown, Belle met Jeannette Rankin who was then chairman of the state's organization for women's suffrage. Belle heard Jeannette speak and from that moment on was a dedicated suffragist (never "suffragette"; that derogatory term was coined by the opposition).

Jeannette spoke on themes familiar to Progressivism, explaining that women needed to vote because government actions directly affected them. For example, Montana's infant and maternity mortality ranked among the nation's highest. Something needed to be done about the

Belle in 1912.

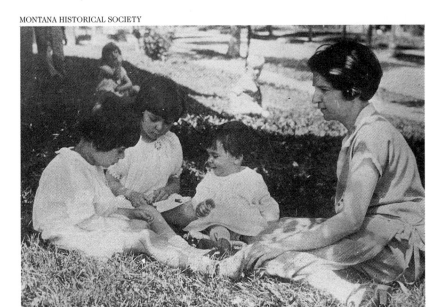

Belle (right) with Judy, Minna and Henry in June 1925.

working conditions of women in factories and industry, and for a healthy population the state needed food and safety inspectors. Opposition to the suffrage movement came from both men and women who felt that it threatened traditional views. As Belle explained it seventy years later, "Women's place was in the home, they said. Women are on a pedestal, why should they come down and mix in 'dirty politics'? Well, we replied, who made politics dirty, and how many of the women who worked in factories or labored on homesteads were on pedestals?"

While Belle's family supported her theories, her mother never got used to her methods. On the corner of what is now Sixth and Park, Belle made the first of many speeches in support of the state suffrage amendment: "Suddenly, it seemed, there was not a soul in sight. But I had something to say, so I just started talking to the world. Miraculously, someone stopped to listen, and soon I had a big audience.... My mother was horrified." No respectable young woman would do such a thing.

Soon Belle was making speeches not only on street corners, but worse, from open automobiles and in front of saloons. Her family became more tolerant until that historic election day in 1914, when someone from Augusta wrote in Belle's name on the ballot for sheriff of Lewis and Clark County. At this, said Belle, "My mother was appalled."

In 1916, after a year as manager and editor of the *Montana Progressive*, Belle resigned (her husband claimed in later years that she was replaced by eight strong men) to help Jeannette Rankin campaign in her bid for the U.S. Senate. When Jeannette won that race, Montana sent the first woman to Congress even before the Nineteenth Amendment (approved in 1920) gave all women the right to vote. Belle accompanied her mentor to Washington as personal secretary and ghost writer for a syndicated newspaper column. In Washington Belle met Norman Winestine, a young Yale graduate destined to become her lifelong friend and soulmate. Norman, who worked for the wartime Food Administration under Herbert Hoover, won Belle's affection by bringing her pies that had been cut open to test for wheat content. They married in April 1918.

Belle's interest in causes continued as she and Norman made their home in Helena. Despite having three children, Belle remained active in politics, lobbying for various causes that ranged from helping to ratify the national child labor amendment to women's right to serve as jurors (won in 1939). With Jeannette Rankin, Dr. Maria Dean and others of the Good Government Clubs (forerunner of the League of Women Voters), Belle helped found the State Vocational School for Girls (now Mountain View), an early result of the full participation of women in Montana politics.

During the Depression, Belle ran for the U.S. Senate under the slogan, "Smaller and Better Senators." She campaigned door-to-door with her children at her side, but was shocked to learn why few would vote for her: she had a husband to support her and didn't need a job. Belle lamented, "I thought running for office was to help somebody."

While equality for women was a lifelong cause for this small-statured champion, it is not the only reason to remember Belle Winestine, who died in 1985. She was a published writer, an artist, a devoted wife and mother, inventor of cardboard picture frames and Kleenex boxes, but more than all of that, she was a lifelong advocate of peace and a friend to many. Those who knew her were fortunate indeed, for, with a characteristic sprig of green in her hair, Belle Winestine truly mastered the craft of living.

CHICAGO JOE

BY LEANNE KURTZ

According to local legend, school administrators concocted Helena's Vigilante Parade to discourage high school seniors from participating in the traditional "Senior Skip Day." Each May, the parade winds its way through downtown Helena with Montana history as the common theme among the assortment of floats assembled by high school students. For those readers who have never had the opportunity to attend or take part in the Vigilante Parade, two things can almost invariably be counted on: 1) The weather will be cold and windy; and 2) Helena's immortal "queen of the underworld," Chicago Joe (also known as Josephine Airey or Josephine Hensley), will make an appearance in one form or another.

Born January 1, 1844, Mary Welch left Ireland at the age of fourteen in hopes of finding fortune and a better life in America. She lived and worked in Chicago's red-light district during the Civil War, and during this period, changed her name to Josephine Airey, a designation much more sophisticated and cultivated than her former. When Josephine arrived in Helena in 1867, the town was teeming with miners and the establishments that supported them. Recognizing the business opportunities in a town full of single men with money to spend, Joe purchased a one-story log building on Wood Street in the heart of Helena's tenderloin and opened her first dance hall.

Also known as "hurdy-gurdy" houses (after the instrument often played in such places), these establishments, in addition to their implied (but rarely spoken) function as brothels, provided entertainment for local men in the form of dancing girls, music, and spirits. Men selected their evening's companions from the array of girls dancing on stage and the only expense to them was the purchase of a drink "for self and lady" at the end of each dance.

Chicago Joe often wore a golden, jewel-studded girdle around her rather massive waist, and prided herself on her "queenly" manner and appearance.

Joe sent away to Chicago for her girls, making sure they were competent dancers and the most attractive in the business. It was this particular practice that earned her the name "Chicago Joe." Her dance hall and bordello met with great success and Joe soon began to acquire more property from which to ply her trade.

In an effort to purify the hearts and minds of the territorial citizenry, the 1885 legislature considered several moral reform measures, among them an anti-gambling law, an age of consent law and an anti–hurdy-gurdy measure. Of these, only the dance hall bill became law. Joe was soon targeted and arrested on the grounds that she operated and refused to close down a hurdy-gurdy. The prosecution's opening statement in the subsequent trial melodramatically described "hurdies" as "establishments wherein men's souls are lured to the shores of sin by the combined seductive influences of wine, women and dance..." Joe was eventually found not guilty after her attorney pointed out (with the help of *Webster's Dictionary*) what exactly a hurdy gurdy was and that no such instrument had ever been spotted in the Red Star Saloon.

On the heels of her victory in court, Joe remodeled a building adjoining the dance hall and created the Coliseum, an ornate variety theater located on Bridge Street (now State Street). The theater featured vaudeville acts backed by electric lighting, elegant fixtures and expensive scenery. Upstairs, Joe installed boxes with heavy curtains providing a relatively private place for clients and employees to "socialize." Each box contained a bell connected to the bar downstairs and the "box girls" as they were now called received commission for the drinks they sold and delivered to the booths.

When the next legislature passed a law that prohibited the sale of liquor in any place frequented by women, Joe responded by cutting a hole into her old dance hall and installing "wine rooms," achieving the same effect, but circumventing the statute, a skill at which she had become exceedingly proficient.

Joe supervised activities nightly at the Coliseum, her large frame heavily jeweled and dressed in a dark velvet robe with a high Elizabethan collar. She often wore a golden, jewel-studded girdle around her rather massive waist, and prided herself on her "queenly" manner and appearance.

All Joe's holdings and her successes in the 1870s and 1880s could not keep her financially solvent when recession hit Helena. Joe borrowed extensively in the early 1890s and finally sold her properties in 1896 for $21,119.23. Joe still owed money to the Thomas Cruse Savings Bank, was taken to court, and when she died in 1899, Joe was virtually penniless.

Given her taste for the ostentatious, Chicago Joe would no doubt relish the idea that her persona is resurrected nearly every year by Helena's high school students. Despite the nature of her business (or perhaps because of it) she remains one of Helena's most successful businesswomen and among the town's most colorful individuals.

Hats off to a Pioneer Educator

By Richard B. Roeder

In our folk history we tend to remember frontier examples of success as measured by wealth and power, men such as copper titans Clark and Daly and cattle barons like Conrad Kohrs. While wealth was an almost universal frontier magnet, many who came west also brought with them the idea that they were agents of civilization destined to transform a wilderness into replicas of the communities they had left behind with institutions such as churches, schools, and fraternal organizations essential to the building and maintaining of a permanent community. These were the civilizers, men and women who have largely been forgotten by us, the beneficiaries of their labors. Many men and women in the story of early Montana deserve recognition as civilizers, but perhaps none does more so than Helena's Cornelius Hedges.

Like so many of his type, Hedges was a New Englander, the son of a Connecticut farmer. Born in 1831, Hedges benefited from an education that was probably the equal of any then available in the country. After preparatory work at Westfield Academy in Massachusetts, Hedges completed bachelor's and master's degrees at Yale and a law degree at Harvard.

Following his education, in 1856 he married and moved with his bride to Iowa in search of new opportunities. There he speculated in real estate, ran a local newspaper, and accumulated debts.

Cornelius Hedges.

In 1864 he left his family in Iowa and went to Alder Gulch seeking the lucky strike that would wipe out his indebtedness and, he hoped, provide real wealth. He was destined for disappointment and had to satisfy himself with manual labor for wages. In 1865 he sought the bonanza again by moving to Last Chance Gulch. He speculated in mining claims (as he did throughout his life) but was never a successful miner and had to depend on his training as a lawyer for an income. Just when Hedges decided that Helena would be his future home is not clear, but in 1867 he brought his wife and two children to Helena. Although real wealth eluded him throughout his life, Hedges was able to combine his law work with elective and appointive offices that enabled him to build a comfortable home on the northwest corner of Rodney and Broadway streets in 1878. Among other positions, Hedges was variously a federal district attorney, probate judge, and Helena city clerk and city attorney. At the same time, he was busy with an almost breathless list of civic activities.

Hedges was best known for his work on behalf of the Masonic Order. His work and writings earned him national recognition within that organization. He was also instrumental in securing construction of the Masonic Home in the Prickly Pear Valley. In addition he helped organize or supported the Helena Public Library, Montana Historical Society, Society of Montana Pioneers, Montana Press Association, Methodist and Presbyterian churches in Helena, and the Helena Board of Trade. He also pioneered the sheep industry, helped organize the Montana Woolgrowers Association in 1895, and was a long-term secretary of the State Board of Sheep Commissioners. He was aided in his support of these numerous activities by his position as a writer for more than thirty years for the *Helena Herald.*

Of all his activities perhaps none has been more important to us as beneficiaries than his four terms as territorial superintendent of public instruction. When Governor Potts first appointed Hedges in 1872, Montana's public schools were poor and few in number. The buildings were generally ramshackle, attendance casual, and teachers poorly prepared. Upon his appointment as superintendent he was able to get the 1872 legislature to adopt a new school law based on that of California that gave him some power over local schools. He personally visited each school at least annually. Under his guidance communities began to build substantial brick buildings, increase attendance requirements, and use standardized texts. Hedges really wanted a normal college to train teachers but had to be satisfied by conducting regular teachers' institutes in each district to improve the preparation of teachers. He also established a teacher certification system based on standardized examinations administered by his office.

Hedges won election as a delegate to the 1884 Constitutional Convention. At the convention he chaired the committee on education and was largely responsible for the education article that was adopted. Although the 1884 Constitution was not used to gain statehood and Hedges was not a delegate in 1889 when statehood was achieved, the 1889 Constitutional Convention adopted almost verbatim his education article of 1884. Truly, with all his civic efforts, Hedges at least deserves to be remembered as the father of Montana's school system. We might also contemplate his idea of the object of public education. Hedges did not regard education in narrow, vocational terms but viewed it in a broad, liberal way whose purpose was to prepare "the next generation to become wiser than their fathers and better fitted to manage the greater interests that will come to their keeping."

Gold Rush Doctors

By Ellen Baumler

Gunshot wounds, mining accidents, spotted fever, cholera, smallpox, measles, respiratory ailments and frostbite created a medical battleground into which courageous gold rush doctors came during the 1860s. The rugged expanse that was Montana Territory offered adventure and limitless opportunity to try out one's medical skills. Both medical school graduates and self-styled doctors with no degree at all came to early Helena for as many reasons as anyone else came west.

Dr. L. Rodney Pococke, a graduate of a St. Louis medical school, was the first doctor to move to Helena permanently. He had no impact on the health of his neighbors since he came not to practice medicine but to combat his own tuberculosis. In slang of the times, Pococke was a "lunger," and hoped the mountain climate would benefit his deteriorating health. The doctor was a first investor in Scott's Addition, choice real estate north of Broadway, but he died before he could realize any profit. Wintering in a poorly chinked cabin brought his demise in the spring of 1865. He was reputedly the first white person to die in Helena, and for that dubious honor Rodney Street was named for him (his last name presumably was too difficult to pronounce).

Dr. Jerome Glick was more dedicated to the profession. The lure of gold initially drew him to Bannack in 1862, but soon his skills earned him a fine reputation as a bone surgeon. One of his most highly acclaimed operations was performed at gunpoint on the infamous Henry Plummer, who had taken a well-aimed bullet in his shooting arm.

In 1865, Dr. Glick formed a partnership in Helena with Dr.

Ira Maupin. The two friends often answered calls together, traveling long distances and operating under the worst possible conditions. Called to Oro Fino one freezing January night, they found three critically wounded gunshot victims lying in the snow. Working by candlelight in a crude cabin, the doctors saved two of the men.

Dr. Glick was highly skilled at setting broken bones and saving limbs, but he also performed many skillful amputations. The doctor amputated the arm of a three-year-old boy within the space of one minute with no anesthetic, and the child apparently felt no pain. Dr. Glick had other famous cases. In 1867 he

Left: Cyrus Stone Ingersoll set up his practice here in 1865 and was Helena's first homeopathic physician. Top: W.L. Steele was called to the scene after the battle of the Big Hole in 1877; he became known as Montana's grand old man of medicine.

removed a seventy-foot tapeworm from a long-suffering patient (the method of removal was not recorded), and in 1873 he cured Army Lt. James H. Bradley of snow blindness.

Dr. Maupin supported Helena's new St. John's Hospital, administering free medical care to the Catholic sisters, referring patients and building up its equipment. Both he and Dr. Glick often drove miles to treat indigent patients. On the way home from such a trip in 1873 Dr. Maupin was thrown from his horse. Helena mourned his death the following day; his patient died three days later. Dr. Glick resumed the practice alone until his death in 1880.

Dr. Cyrus S. Ingersoll, Helena's first homeopathic physician, set up practice in 1865. Disdain for the strong medicines prescribed by his contemporaries won him a large clientele, among them many women and children. Dr. Ingersoll was a skilled surgeon and successfully handled many stabbings and mine accidents. His care and concern went beyond the usual: he once accompanied a smallpox victim to the pesthouse and remained several weeks to oversee recovery.

Montana's "grand old man of medicine," Dr. William L. Steele, was a key contributor not only to Helena's early health care, but also to the community at large. He arrived at Last Chance in 1864 and served as county sheriff and treasurer, ten years as coroner, three terms as mayor and as a state legislator.

Dr. Steele had an exceptional reputation as a surgeon and diagnostician. He won renown in 1877 after the battle of the Big Hole when he and other doctors were called to the scene. Long into the night, Helena teamster Hugh Kirkendall held the patients while surgeons operated by lamplight without benefit of chloroform or ether.

Dr. Steele's services as an obstetrician were in great demand among both settlers and Native Americans. He was contemplating the difficult birth of a Piegan patient when a colleague expressed the common opinion that "an Indian woman went into the bushes when her time came and managed delivery…" Dr. Steele replied, "They have just as hard [a] time as their white sisters and many never come out…"

Dr. Steele was called to see Mrs. Rouch, an eccentric dairy

owner who dressed like a man and never bathed. Upon examining her sprained ankle which she had just washed in hot water, Dr. Steele declared, "This is the dirtiest damn foot in Montana!" Mrs. Rouch bet him $5 to the contrary and removed her other boot. She won the bet.

At the close of 1866, many medical men had passed through Helena. Drs. Glick, Maupin, Ingersoll, Steele and a few others who stayed made a difference to hundreds and hundreds of early community residents. For many years one grateful pioneer remembered Dr. Steele with a box of cigars every Christmas. Musing over the gift in 1901, Dr. Steele observed, "The giver says I saved her life when she was small. I don't know. Maybe I did."

J.S.M.
NEILL

BY HARRIETT C.
MELOY

FROM JACK CORY SKETCH,
MONTANA CLUB SMOKER
INVITATION 1905

John Hakola's engrossing doctoral thesis on the life and times of Samuel T. Hauser begins with the assertion that study of business leaders' lives is a relatively neglected field of Western historiography. Hakola then corrects the Hauser problem by writing a 300-leaf dissertation.

But what about biographical studies of other early entrepreneurs?

Helenans, at the turn of the 20th century, evidently recognized the value of men who advanced our city's economic and social affairs. One way they honored prominent men was to name streets for them. This article is about the man whose name was given to one of the city's shortest thoroughfares, Neill Avenue, the street that passes the Civic Center and stretches between Benton Avenue and Last Chance Gulch.

John Neill was perceived by his peers to be a master builder, a hard worker with natural ability, who dedicated his life to promoting the interests of state and community while improving his own personal fortune. He was, in fact, a friend of the more famous Hauser though the older man was at least thirty years Neill's senior and past his productive prime when Neill came on the scene. In at least one remarkable enterprise that, sadly, did not succeed, they were collaborators. The entrepreneurial tie that related the two is obvious to anyone reading numerous letters they exchanged around the turn of the century. (Helena's longest street, beginning at Getchell and extending to the city's western edge, was named for Samuel Hauser, Territorial Governor from 1885 to 1887.)

Forty years before 1900, March 25, 1860, John Selby Martin Neill was born in St. Paul, Minnesota, the son of Rev. Edward D. and Nancy (Hall) Neill. When John was nine years old his father was appointed to the consulship of Ireland by President Grant. After the family's sojourn in Ireland, they returned to the United States where John attended Delaware College at Newark, Delaware, earning a B.A. degree. Two years later he studied law at Columbian University, Washington, D.C., before moving to Helena in 1883.

Before leaving for Montana, Neill married Margaret Evans, daughter of George Gillespie Evans and Mary Black Evans of Newark, New Jersey. On October 30, 1884, a son, George Gillespie Evans Neill was born to the couple. Shortly after the baby's birth, Margaret and son followed John to Helena.

Before coming to Montana, Neill, a Democrat, worked for the election of Grover Cleveland, who became United States President in 1884. As a reward for his services, the president appointed John Neill surveyor general of Montana, a position he held until Cleveland was defeated.

In the early 1890s, Neill purchased the *Helena Independent,* thus assuring the newspaper's strong future support of Democrats. Always a powerful advocate for Democratic doctrine, Neill actively promoted the careers of numerous politicians: W.A. Clark, T.J. Walsh, S.T. Hauser, E.L. Norris and J.K. Toole. Neill was a "prime mover" in W.A. Clark's bid for the U.S. Senate. Neill never ran for a political office, nor did he make political speeches, but when challenged to speak about certain issues in which he had a passionate interest, he "arose to his feet to pour forth a stream of direct and powerful words that overpowered his adversaries," according to a close friend, E.C. Day.

While maintaining interest in Democratic politics, Neill also directed attention to local civic improvement in coordination with his ever expanding real-estate business. Sanders' *History of Montana,* (1913) gives credit to Neill for "planning of some of Helena's most remarkable achievements," including the "Mount Helena forest park, the LeGrande Cannon boulevard and the west side improvement district." Plans for "a greater state fair" were attributed to Neill. In 1909, he organized a committee to improve the Fairgrounds, which needed a new grandstand and buildings to display animals; both goals were reached within a year and a half. He also raised money for the building of the largest and best hotel in the region—the Placer. And along with Thomas A. Marlow, Neill was influential in obtaining funding to construct the Marlow Theater.

While Neill and Hauser expended energy and brainpower for the good of Montana and Helena, their personal fortunes suffered severely during the Silver Panic of 1893. Hoping to recover their losses as well as benefit Helena and Butte, Hauser and Neill combined forces to attempt an unusually ambitious project, the Rapid Transit interurban electric rail line between the capital city and the mining city. Joined by other prominent Montanans, the two entrepreneurs planned to construct and promote the line.

The confident promoters believed that "heavy steam trains are not adapted to making quick runs on mountain grades" and that the customary three- to four-hour travel time between Helena and Butte could be reduced appreciably by installing the electric line. Another cause for optimism was the "low price of electric power."

Naturally, fuel to propel the line was to come from Hauser's electric plants on the Missouri River.

But the project failed for at least two reasons. One obstacle was the Great Northern Railway, a line already carrying passengers and freight successfully, albeit slowly, between Helena and Butte. The other deterrent was lack of interest by financiers to fund the huge endeavor.

Seldom dissuaded by any setback, visionaries such as Neill, Hauser, Broadwater and many others turned their backs on failure and pressed on to improve life for their fellow citizens and themselves as well. Neill died in 1912, leaving a legacy of notable improvements for Helena. The least Helena could do was name a street for him.

Numerous Helena streets were named to honor men who contributed to our city's economic and social advancement. While Neill Avenue is one of the shortest of these roadways, one of the longest is Hauser Boulevard, which begins at Getchell and ends at the western edge of Helena.

CASTING MYTH BACK TO REALITY: THE DEATH OF PAUL MACLEAN

BY ELLEN BAUMLER

Most Helenans have read Norman Maclean's novella *A River Runs Through It* or seen Robert Redford's 1991 movie. The moderately fictionalized autobiographical story by this one-time Helena resident was published in 1976 along with two other stories about Maclean's youth. Rejected by all the major publishers until taken on by the prestigious University of Chicago Press, it was singled out by the Pulitzer Prize fiction jury as the year's best fiction. The Pulitzer advisory board, however, declined to confer an award that year.

Norman Maclean, who died at the age of 87 in 1990, began writing at age 70 after retirement from the University of Chicago classroom. A lifetime of fishing in Montana and teaching (Shakespeare, no less) well prepared him to spin a fact-based fishing story into an eloquent, critically acclaimed "mini-epic." His brother, Paul, is the hero whose artistic perfection as a fly fisherman sets him apart. Maclean-as-writer, however, bestows flaws upon this character that explain his violent death: he drinks too much, he gambles to a fault, he takes too many chances, and he refuses to be helped. What truth did Maclean cast into this ill-fated character?

In the late '20s and early '30s, the Maclean family lived in Helena in a modest home in the 800 block of Broadway. Reverend Maclean retired from the pulpit in 1925 to head the Montana Presbyterian Church Synod and the family moved here

Above: Two unidentified reporters in the newsroom of The
Independent *circa 1930.*
*Top: Junction of the Clearwater and Blackfoot rivers—a
favorite haunt of the Macleans.*

from Missoula. Their two sons, Norman and Paul, were then 22 and 19. Norman had received his degree from Dartmouth at Hanover, New Hampshire, and Paul was still a student. It is true that Norman and Paul were fighters and daredevils; some Helena residents still remember their antics.

Both book and movie emphasize Paul's love of Montana as well as his gambling, drinking and penchant for taking risks. These "story facts" culminate in the nonspecific circumstances surrounding his death, which we are led to believe occurred in Montana. In both the book and movie he tells Norman, "I'll never leave Montana." In fact, Paul Maclean did leave the state more than once, and he died in Chicago.

Following his brother's lead, Paul graduated from Dartmouth (not the University of Montana, as in the movie), and taught English there for a year before returning to Montana where he worked for the *Montana Record-Herald*, the *Great Falls Leader* and the *Great Falls Tribune*. Hired as statehouse reporter for *The Independent* in 1932, Paul gained a fine reputation in Helena as a reporter covering the legislative sessions of 1933, 1935 and 1937 (not, as reported in the movie, covering the "crime beat"). In March of 1937, he took a position with the University of Chicago's press relations bureau. Norman was teaching there, and Paul continued his studies in English. He was to receive his master's degree in June 1938.

On May 3, 1938, the Helena paper carried the Chicago account of events occurring there in the early morning hours of the previous day. A resident heard sounds of a scuffle in the alley at the rear of his home. An hour later, he went outside to find a man lying unconscious. An empty wallet and cigarette case were lying near the victim. Paul Maclean never regained consciousness. He sustained a severe basal skull fracture and bruising on the forehead (as from a club). Multiple bruises on his body were evidence that he "...had battled fiercely with his assailants." Authorities leaned toward robbery, but circumstances indicated other possible motives. A house-to-house search was to no avail and a coroner's inquest, held the next morning, yielded no further information. There were no arrests and the case was never solved.

Terry Dwyer, former managing editor of the *Great Falls*

Tribune, worked for the *Independent Record* following World War II when the Maclean tragedy was still fairly fresh. In a recent *Tribune* editorial, Dwyer recalls that men who knew Paul remembered him as intemperate, impatient with racial slurs and "...a man who would not back away from a barroom brawl, regardless of the odds." Despite this, he was professionally respected as a "good newsman." According to Dwyer, some of Paul's former Helena associates believed that his murder was mob related, that perhaps the reporter stumbled upon information that warranted permanent silencing. Dwyer goes on to speculate that given the low pay levels of the '30s, it would not be difficult to be in debt. If Paul had been in debt, it would not necessarily have been from gambling. In 1977, Norman Maclean said of the murder in an interview with the *New York Times*, "...we never understood how or why, and I was never able to assimilate his death."

In 1986, before the movie rights were settled, the *Los Angeles Times* reported that actor William Hurt had traveled to Montana to fish with the author. After the two finished casting their lines, Hurt asked if he was good enough to play Paul. Maclean replied, "You're a pretty good fisherman, Bill, but not good enough to be my brother." Clearly, Maclean remembered Paul as an incomparable artist.

Jean Maclean Snyder several years ago told the *Livingston Enterprise* that her father "...believed you come to terms with something...by understanding it..." After half a lifetime, Norman Maclean finally came to terms with this tragedy by casting his brother, the expert fly fisherman, as an artist and a hero, supplying answers to long-unanswered questions that, in truth, probably do not have answers. The book was his first public discussion of the family tragedy and did not come easy. Maclean confessed, "I was almost afraid to sleep, afraid I'd lose the connections..." Dredging up the past and supplying answers brought the author great personal anguish. The novella, then, truly came about according to the dictum set forth in *River* by Maclean's minister-father: "All good things...come by grace and grace comes by art and art does not come easy."

LIFESTYLE

GRAND & GLORIOUS HOLIDAY FARE

❦

BY LEANNE KURTZ

As we prepare for our annual holiday feasts, set the table, put the miniature marshmallows on our canned yams, and give thanks for the spread laid out before us, perhaps we should also be giving thanks that boiled opossum, ox tongue and sauté of calf's brains are not included on the menu. Late-19th-century Helenans were not so lucky—although they considered themselves so—as the dishes mentioned above and many other strange concoctions were standard holiday bill of fare at many local restaurants. Turkey has long been the mainstay of holiday dining, but side dishes and alternatives to the popular fowl have changed tremendously through time, as have our eating habits and tastes.

Many consider life in early Helena and the West as austere and exacting, with miners, cowboys and homesteaders barely eking out a living, making do with hard tack, beans and coffee. That was indeed the way many early settlers of the West survived, but local area restaurant menus and grocery store advertisements from the late 1800s tell a different story. Dining truly presented a smorgasbord of exotic flavors, for those with the stomach for it.

The foods served in restaurants and in local homes in the

*As they wait for the camera lens to click in this portrait of a
Jewish family dinner, these early Helenans look fairly
stiff...maybe they're thinking of the fine fare before them.*

1880s and 1890s would likely have sent modern physicians
reeling as cholesterol content readings leaped off the charts.
"Lite" was not an option and lard was used in everything and
used so frequently that it sold in 100-pound cases. Calorie-
conscious folks and vegetarians would have been hard-pressed
to find much to their liking among the dishes offered.

On Thanksgiving Day in 1894, the Helena Cafe served dinner from 12 to 8 o'clock. For fifty cents per person, fortunate
patrons were treated to Mock Turtle Soup (no turtles involved),
Barbecue of Smelts, Sauté of Calf's Brains, the obligatory tur-

key, lobster salad, various meat options, and English Plum Pudding with brandy sauce. Fifty cents seemed to be the going rate for Christmas dinner in 1897 at the Capital Restaurant, located at 105 North Main Street. Here the menu consisted of Fresh Beef Tongue in Tomato Sauce, a relish called "Chow-Chow" (I am assuming this is *not* of the canine variety), and Steamed Suet Pudding with brandy sauce. It must truly have been a work of magic to convert suet into a palatable dish. Other special holiday menus at the Helena Cafe and the Capital Restaurant included such exquisite edibles as Ox Tongue Jardiniere, Beef Heart in Tomato Sauce, Chicken Giblet Pie, Ox Tongue Piquant, and Croquettes of Sweetbreads (a.k.a. the thymus or pancreas of a calf) au Mushrooms. Of course early Helenans didn't have the option of "Stove Top Stuffing instead of Sweetbreads..."

Opossum seemed to be a popular item in early Helena. Although the area has not been known for its abundance of opossum, the little rat-like marsupial managed to find its way to many a local dinner table. The African Methodist Episcopal church even hosted an annual "Opossum Feed" as a fund raiser for the congregation. The main course had to be imported from points south so its appearance was cause for a celebratory feast.

Before arrival of the railroad in the Helena area, most supplies either endured the 465-mile journey from Corrine, Utah, the terminus of the Union Pacific line, or ventured down the Missouri aboard a steamboat. The wagon haul faced obvious impediments and delays and the steamboats had to navigate numerous rapids and sand bars simply to reach Fort Benton. When one considers the number of hazards facing a wagon driver or steamboat operator filled to the brink with supplies crossing a still-wild countryside, it is easy to see how prices must have drastically fluctuated, resulting in the need for daily publication of California fruit and vegetable prices.

An April 1898 price list for Lindsay & Co., a Helena wholesale dealer in "fruits, produce, grass and clover seeds," featured oranges, lemons, grapefruit, apples, bananas, and an assortment of California vegetables. Oysters were shipped in 50-gallon barrels into which the hapless storekeeper would often have to reach deep to portion out the slimy delicacies for customers. Among the items on the price list, Lindsay & Co. warned that onion sets and turkeys, particularly, were "very scarce." Canned Lunch Tongue, Pickled Pigs Feet and Canned Chicken Tamales lined the shelves at the Lindsay and Co. store. Hungry Helenans could purchase a pound of Canned Lunch Tongue for $5.50. Apparently, it was worth every penny! And depending on the markets and the season, oranges could cost as much as a dollar apiece. The fresh California fruits and vegetables that we often take for granted were a rare treat in the off-season and many people resorted to dried versions of the real thing.

Knowing what we do now about the bacteria and contamination in poorly prepared foods, primarily meat, it seems incredible that the human race has survived as long as it has. As late as the 1930s, a local turkey farmer would simply wash the bird's head and feet upon its demise, roll it in paper and ship it off to Chicago, innards still intact. With its viscera in place, dealers claimed, the turkey looked bigger and plumper—never mind the gruesome task that awaited the consumer.

So put all of this out of your mind as you sit down to commemorate our country's day of giving thanks for all that we have. Enjoy the green-bean casserole with the french-fried onions on top, the Butterball with the built-in thermometer and the low-cal pumpkin pie topped with Cool Whip "lite." Thank your host and thank the cosmos that opossum stay in the south and that suet has been retired as a dish for human consumption. Leave it for the birds.

HELENA
HARMONY

BY ELLEN BAUMLER

*Not the brain child of one individual, Helena's band is
the musical production of several musicians, who
found harmony more enjoyable than solos. Born in a
mining camp, the band was reared in the age of the
Sunday afternoon concert; it served in two world
wars; it suffered tragedies of financial insecurity and
decaying enthusiasm; it thrived with excellent members; it mellowed with time and matured a solid citizen of Helena.*
                                   Independent Record, *August 10, 1952*

From its earliest days as a mining camp, Helena has been
blessed with many more than its share of talented musicians.
In the days before recordings and radio, live music was an essential part of entertainment. Vaudeville players and professional musicians who regularly played at the Ming Opera House,
in Central Park (northwest of the Green Meadow Country Club,
along Ten Mile Creek), or at the many saloons and "palaces"
were from an early date organized into various other bands,
orchestras and ensembles. One of these loosely organized
groups was an impromptu city band that played unrehearsed
for political rallies, Fourth of July parades, and other civic gatherings.

Among the many musicians who played a key role in Helena's musical past and its city band was Minnesota-born Jake
Zimmerman. He arrived in Helena in 1890, having completed
studies in bookkeeping and commercial law. Jake had longed
to be a professional musician, but his family considered that

an unsuitable profession. In Helena he was able to realize this dream by obtaining fairly steady work playing in several different orchestras.

One of the groups that initially employed Jake was Madame Marie Ericke's Bohemian Orchestra. Madame, a native

Set-up for the Minstrel Show in the Old Ming Theater, 1893–1895.

of Germany and noted violinist, had played before European royalty. She came to Helena in the 1890s with her musician-husband, Ernst, and was an immediate sensation: "many big deals were consummated to the seductive melodies...and the haunting strains of her violin." Madame, Ernst and Jake formed a long association, collaborating on many projects. The three of them had a hand in organizing and arranging music for most of Helena's early musical groups. Although it seemed that Madame Ericke and Jake Zimmerman began to follow different professional directions, their lives continued to be intertwined.

By the late 1890s, Jake had learned a great deal from his association with the Erickes. He rallied the sometime city band, took up the baton and embarked upon the project that would span his lifetime. Jake's city band, however, soon faced its first crisis when an international pitch was established. Band members discovered that their instruments were "as outmoded as a hoopskirt and a Confederate collar." American instruments had previously been manufactured at "concert pitch," which was based on a higher number of vibrations per second than the new standard. Three years and many benefit dances later, the band was able to purchase $3,000 worth of new instru-

Handbill advertising performance of March 23, 1895. VERTICAL FILES/ MONTANA HISTORICAL SOCIETY LIBRARY

ments at the lower pitch. It was the first in Montana to do so.

The thirty-five members incorporated in 1902 as the State Capital Band. Well-equipped and well-rehearsed, the band began summer concerts on the lawn of the courthouse, where the audience sometimes swelled to 3,000. Band members included the Houle brothers, Al Rinda, Joe Seiler, John Adami, Dr. J.A. Gordon, Archie Beaupre and the Erickes' son, Billie.

Meanwhile, Jake boarded with the Erickes at their home on Harrison Avenue where Madame ran a music studio, gave lessons and rehearsed her several orchestras. One of them was comprised of all women. "No social affair was a complete success" without Madame and her violin. Madame Ericke's Orchestra also played at Mrs. Sulgrove's Dance Academy, where most of Helena's youth learned their way around a ballroom. (Mrs. Sulgrove, incidentally, required all boys to wear one glove so as not to dirty the back of his partner's dress.)

Just as the State Capital Band was developing a good repertoire and a better reputation, the government placed the Twenty-fourth Infantry Band, an expert polished group, at Fort Harrison. The hometown group felt the stiff competition and membership began to dwindle. When the Twenty-fourth left a few years later, Helena was again without a band.

In 1914, A.I. "Daddy" Reeves took strict control as manager of the State Capital Band, demanding, to the horror of its members, two practice sessions a week. Jake remained as the competent director, leading a spectacular concert in 1915 that came to be known as the "greatest band event in the history of Helena." The following year, Jake Zimmerman—whom everyone had thought a confirmed bachelor at age fifty-one—quietly married Madame Ericke. Ernst had died quite suddenly of apparent heart failure in 1913.

World War I took many band members away from the home front, and Jake Zimmerman resigned in 1921 because of ill health. A few months later, the self-taught musician/arranger died suddenly at age fifty-six, after seeming to take a turn for the better. His legacy included more than two decades of service to his band and a musical library celebrated as the most complete in the Northwest.

Madame Ericke-Zimmerman continued to lead her orchestra and teach her students. She outlived yet a third husband and died in 1943. According to her obituary, she had once been a beauty, but died "a broken little old lady" surrounded by treasures of the past that included a Stradivarius violin. Years after, her name "was spoken in hushed tones, not for the fate of her...husbands, but as the revered teacher" of hundreds of Helena's aspiring young musicians.

Helena's musical history is further indebted to J.B. "Jack" Mason who helped revive the city band in the 1920s. This self-taught musician did a lot more than play trumpet in his sixty years with the group. Thanks to his meticulous collecting, 4,000 pieces of music from Helena groups and elsewhere (including the Zimmerman-Ericke collection) are now safely housed at the Montana State Historical Society's library.

Although Madame Ericke's Orchestra died with its leader, the State Capital Band plays on today, giving free weekly concerts during the summer. Dedicated band members range from high school students to retirees and well deserve community appreciation for maintaining this harmonious tradition.

Thanks to Montana Historical Society librarian Bob Clark for sharing his research and notes.

HOGMANAY! AND HAPPY NEW YEAR

BY CHERE JIUSTO

Old-time Helenans enjoyed holidays and celebrated them in high style. And they were just as interested in the origins of these celebrations then, as we are today. Stories published in the 1870s *Helena Herald* described New Year's celebrations of Olde England and Scotland, tracing back to the 18th century:

The last day of the year is called in Scotland Hogmanay, a word which has fruitlessly exercised the wits of the etymologists. The Scottish people, overlooking Christmas in obedience to the behests of their religious teachers have transferred the merriment of the season to Hogmanay and New Year's day, which they accordingly abandon to all kinds of festivity. Handsel Monday, or the first Monday of the year, the children in small towns perambulate among the neighbors of the better class, crying at their doors, "Hogmanay!" or, sometimes the following rhyme:

Hogmanay, tollolay.
Gie's of your white bread and none of your gray.

In obedience to which call they are served each with an oaten cake. In the evening there are merry makings, which are always prolonged to twelve o'clock, which has no sooner struck than all start up excitedly and wish each other a happy new year. Small, venturous parties take a kettle with hot ale passet, called a "het pint, and go to the houses of their friends to wish them a happy new year. Whoever comes first is called in that home, "The First Foot"; and it is deemed necessary on such occasions, to offer the inmates both a piece of cake and a sip from the passet kettle, otherwise, they would not be lucky throughout the year. This is familiarly called, "First Footing."

⁂

Next day, all people go about among all other peoples homes; presents are given among relations and dinner parties closed the evening. Formerly, the first Monday of the year was also observed as a festive day and time for giving presents, from which latter circumstance it was called Handsel Monday. The Handsel Monday, old style, is still, in some rural districts, the chief feast day of the season. On the evenings of Christmas, Hogmanay, New Year's Day and Handsel Monday, parties of young men and boys went about disguised in old shirts and paper vizards, singing at the various houses for a small guerdon.

⁂

In New York and other Eastern and Western cities, the custom of "Calling" on New Year's Day, and keeping "open house" has of late years obtained very general popularity....Young ladies receive calls from gentlemen on that day and feast them with wine, choice fruits and luxuries of all kinds.

Indeed, open houses were the order of the day in Helena a century ago. Drawing upon those European roots, people across Helena opened their houses to callers, friends and relatives, and New Year's revelers would jump into carriages that were "turned out" in holiday finery for visits around the town.

Fine "turnouts" were a matter of pride and craft for local livery stables, who teamed up horses with sleighs and bells to whisk the callers on their appointed rounds. The newspapers often remarked upon the most "dashy and luxurious" rigs, such as a "most notable and attractive... six-in-hand mule team outfit, with gold mounted harness, driver, footman and other at-

Old-time greeting card.

tendants." The sleigh was reportedly "one of the most stylish in the city" and conveyed "four of our most prominent and popular young men, elegantly dressed" and each wearing "a brand new black silk hat."

While the press lauded the festive carriages and challenged any "turnouts" in cities back east to rival those in the "go ahead city of Helena," they frowned sternly upon the holiday excesses of some callers who became noticeably smashed by the end of a long day of calling. Serving liquor to gentleman callers "is a most vicious custom and should be supplanted," stated one writer of the day.

Of course each New Year's celebration was launched at the strike of midnight, and in addition to much libation, was never complete without fireworks and noisemakers. One hundred years ago, as the big clock chimed on the county courthouse, steeple bells pealed and steam whistles blared, soldiers from Fort Harrison blew off a howitzer in town and a squad of gunmen on the roof of the Power Block fired several volleys of ammunition. "Besides these, every one who owned a pistol or a gun thought it his place to help celebrate and it is not a big estimate to say that over a thousand shots were fired in all."

Each year, as the smoke clears from the ringing in of the new, let us join together in the spirit of the season and the new year, wishing Hogmanay! to one and all.

On the Air

BY LEANNE
KURTZ

From its inception, radio has played a critical role in 20th century American society. Those of us who grew up with television have all heard the stories of families crowded around the radio, listening to news reports during wartime, laughing with Red Skelton, and panicking when reports of invading Martians flooded the airwaves. The radio became the focal point of many American living rooms and Montanans were no exception.

On September 27, 1937, the *Helena Independent* published a small announcement informing the public that a new radio station would begin broadcasting on October 1. On schedule, the People's Forum of the Air (KPFA) commenced operations at 1210 on the dial.

The station originally operated from the Pittsburgh block on Main Street (a building demolished in 1970). In its first few days, KPFA offered recordings of President Roosevelt's speech from Chicago, and an address by U.S. Supreme Court Justice Black during the controversy over his affiliation with the Ku Klux Klan. The station's October 7 broadcast included "Art Chappelle and his Accordion," and Governor Ayers' speech from the Placer Hotel. K.O. MacPherson, KPFA's station manager boasted to listeners, "KPFA is *your* station—dedicated to serve you—a station which will at all times disseminate information to you without censorship of any kind."

Local advertisers quickly took advantage of the new medium. In a letter to the station in 1938, the owner of Helena's A.P. Curtin Co. claimed the company sold $1,500 worth of furniture in a one-day sale, thanks to its commercial on KPFA. Other frequent advertisers included S.C. Smither's Shoe Company and the Helena Chrysler dealers.

In November 1938, *The Billboard,* a national periodical, featured the results of a Helena radio survey. Least popular among the programs included "Montana Slim," "Agriculture Today," and "National Hillbilly Champions." Helenans seemed to prefer "Texaco News," football games and a serial called "Affairs of Anthony." The *Billboard* article noted that the Helena dailies had been unfriendly to this intrusive new medium. The *Helena Independent* and the *Montana Record-Herald,* according to *The Billboard,* have no radio departments, are "not friendly to radio; will not mention any station names in columns. Will not use anything of publicity nature if touched by radio."

During its years on the air, KPFA's call letters were changed to KXLJ, joining the rest of the "XL" family forming what was known as the Z Bar Network, a name derived from a famous Montana cattle brand. Z Bar included KXLF in Butte, KXLQ in Bozeman, KXLK in Great Falls and KXLL in Missoula.

KXLJ took pride in its programming and its contributions to the community. The station featured amateur broadcasts of local high-school students and aired legislative highlights. In December 1942, KXLJ's programming schedule included: Red Skelton, radio's "Bad Widdle Boy"; an installment of "The Aldrich Family" in which "Henry Aldrich shovels most of Centerville out of the snow in a circuitous search for a gift for his best girl, Kathleen"; "Mr. District Attorney" cracking The Case of the Zoot Suit Killer; and "Maxwell House Coffee Time" featuring Baby Snooks.

A 1942 program to promote the sale of war bonds preempted several of KXLJ's regularly scheduled shows, including the popular "Catholic Hour." An irate listener wrote the station protesting preemption of her favorite show. The listener complained that "there are so many unbearable programs that we have to turn off anyway..."

In 1949, KXLJ got its first dose of competition with the birth of another radio station in Helena, and it wouldn't be long before television made its appearence. By the late 1950s, Helena TV, Inc., was formed and by 1959, KXLJ-TV was on the air.

Even with the advent of TV and its increasing popularity, radio continues to thrive. It is nearly inconceivable (but sort of fun) to imagine the effect a Howard Stern or a Rush Limbaugh would have had on Helenans in the 1930s and 1940s. Citizens of the Queen City were shocked when a local broadcaster, thinking he was off the air uttered an obscenity that made headlines in the March 12, 1938, edition of the *Helena Independent.* The article, entitled "Naughty; Did Nice Radio Man Say Bad Word?" gleefully explained that many citizens "who were not only shocked but angered" called the *Independent* reporting they had heard the ace of profanity, "You son of a _ _ _ _ _." The *Independent* recounted:

> *There was sweet music issuing from their loud speakers. Then the music broke off suddenly. As they turned to look at their radios, a man's gruff voice snarled, 'Now look what you've done you dizzy _ _ _ _, etc.'*

That announcer no doubt learned how to better use his equipment, and horrified Helenans, once they recovered from the jolt, turned their radios back on just in time to catch "Those Happy Gillmans."

Sliding
on Slats

❧❀❧

BY LEANNE
KURTZ

Remember when winter in Helena meant snow? I don't mean a squall here and there. I'm talking that week-long, waist-high, school-closing, traffic-stopping, tie-a-rope-around-your-waist-so-you-don't-get-lost-on-the-way-to-the-barn kind of snow for which Montana is notorious. While many locals welcome the balmy temperatures and clear streets that have become the winter norm for the past few years, hearty winter recreation enthusiasts are no doubt mourning those frosty seasons of yesteryear when a good pair of hickory skis cost $12 and Chaucer Street provided members of the Mount Helena Ski Club some vertical drop and enough snow to practice their turns.

Although Helenans were quick to pick up on the relatively new sport of skiing, consensus is that Anaconda witnessed the dawn of organized skiing in Montana. In the early 1930s, Anaconda's Chamber of Commerce brought to town Casper Oeman, a Norwegian ski jumper, in an effort to attract visitors. Oeman provided jumping demonstrations in Sheeps Gulch behind the Anaconda courthouse and within a few years, enthusiasm for sliding down a mountain on wooden boards had infected Helena area thrill-seekers.

Spearheaded by Turner Clack, a local ski devotee, recreationalists organized themselves in January of 1937, forming the Mount Helena Ski Club. The mountain for which the club was named became a popular haunt, as did Mount Ascension, MacDonald Pass, Unionville, McLellan Creek, Blossburg, and the snow-blanketed streets of town. In its first year, members undertook the clearing of trails on Mount Ascension and Mount Helena, installed lights at the foot of Ascension, and sponsored ski trains to a run at Blossburg, a railroad siding on Mullan Pass Road. With membership dues, the club provided the Helena area with its first ski tow and a chalet at Mason's Basin, just west of the top of MacDonald Pass, a welcome relief to those who preferred gliding downhill to hiking uphill. The Rimini Mine contributed materials for the 1,000-foot tow, which ran on a Buick motor and pulled five people per minute to the top of the course.

In 1941, the motor-powered tow on MacDonald Pass was replaced by an overhead electric tow, the ski run was lighted, and the chalet equipped with a telephone and furniture, all for a little over $1,000. Carpenters donated their time, and much of the equipment needed for the improvements came without cost to the club. When the National Ski Association president visited the Helena club, he remarked that members were among the most enthusiastic he had encountered in the country. Perhaps due in part to members' passion for the sport, the Mount Helena Ski Club was made host of the 1942 Northern Rocky Mountain Ski Races.

The MacDonald Pass course was not long enough or steep enough to adequately challenge the caliber of racers who would be arriving for the tournament. Club members set out in the spring of 1940 to locate the perfect arena for the event. After a strenuous tour of the sizable mountains in the area (Elkhorn, Baldy, Red Mountain, Edith, and Belmont), club members decided upon Mount Belmont as the site for the upcoming tournament, citing its 1,700-foot vertical drop, its accessibility, and the deep snow, which had lasted until May the previous year. Mount Belmont, known to Marysville miners as Mount Pleasant, had occasionally been trod upon by skiers, as roads in the area were usually hard packed by horses and equipment servicing the mines. Unemployed miners helped clear the trails and the mountain assumed the name of one of the numerous mines that dotted the area. The run established for the tournament began at the top of Mount Belmont and ended a quarter of a mile from the end of Marysville's main street. Residents of Marysville welcomed the new industry to their town, and predicted that with the incursion of skiers, their little burg might soon be transformed from a mining community into a destination ski resort.

Not surprisingly, America's involvement in World War II sharply curtailed skiing, as it did most recreational pursuits. Gas was at a premium and many of the young people who participated in the sport were defending their country across the Atlantic. The Mount Helena Ski Club's focus turned from rec-

Skiing Mount Belmont.

reation to assisting in the war effort. Members advised the army in its formation of mountain troops, a branch to be "equipped and drilled to battle in rugged areas where operations are difficult for average troops." The army asked ski clubs all over the country for assistance in training soldiers and ensuring that experienced guides would be available should mountain warfare in the United States become a reality.

Fortunately, the local alpine guides were not needed, and in the winter of 1946, skiers were again ready to take to the hills. As a Forest Service official told a reporter in the fall of 1946, "We believe this season, the first post-war period when everyone will have full opportunity to revel in winter sports, will find more persons availing themselves of the area's incomparable advantages than ever before." Skiers returned to Mount Belmont, where they were greeted by two rope tows and a lodge. Patrons were welcome to spend the night at the lodge, provided they were equipped with blankets and sleeping bags.

Ski clothing and the necessary gear have certainly come a long way in the last sixty years. Before the days of lightweight Patagonia underwear, waterproof anoraks, quick release bindings and high-tech Rossignols, there were hickory and maple

skis, cable bindings, heavy wool parkas, leather boots and gabardine "trousers." As is true today, however, high-performance fashion was considered vital to the overall experience. White Stag advertised that all of their "togs" were "ski tested by 'Skier Stylists'" the year before they hit the stores. A White Stag advertisement in the *Helena Record-Herald* reads "The Smartest Ski Outfits on the Marysville Run Reflects all the 'know' of the White Stag Skier Stylist; has the lines, the details, the color appeal!" The picture features a larger-than-life woman gripping her skis, gazing boldly into the distance, sporting her White Stag "Logger Jack" ensemble.

In the midst of the second brown winter in as many years in the Helena area, it is looking like cold, snowy, rugged Montana winters have gone the way of the $18 Sears ski package, the $9 parka, and use of the word "togs." Although Marysville never did become that destination resort, local skiers can still get their fix on Mount Belmont, at the area now known as the Great Divide. Three chair lifts, the first of which was installed in 1986, haul skiers all over the old mining territory, offering numerous opportunities, as a reporter put it in 1946, for "breaking one's neck on a pair of slats." The mountain seems to catch the snow that does arrive in the area, and although you can't spend the night on the floor of the lodge anymore, at least you don't have to hike to the top in gabardine wool trousers.

Newspapers of the Black Community

BY LEANNE KURTZ

In September 1894, a new newspaper began publication in Helena; its aim was to promote the "social, moral and industrial interests" of its readership. With its first issue, the paper jumped headlong into the political fracas between Anaconda and Helena for designation as the state's capital. Unmistakably Republican, the paper devoted numerous editorials and articles during its brief life to disparaging Marcus Daly and the Anaconda Copper Company. In its first issue, the editorial staff expressed "hope that our people throughout the state without exception will speak a good word for Helena as the permanent capital and on the 6th of November next vote for the city where five hundred of us live." The "us" to which the paper referred was Helena's black community,

Joseph B. Bass.
MONTANA HISTORICAL SOCIETY

and the paper was known as *The Colored Citizen*, one of two Helena newspapers between 1894 and 1911 published by and devoted to the interests of Helena's black community.

Census records indicate that in 1910 Helena's black population numbered 420. From this stable and prosperous community, church groups, fraternal organizations and social clubs formed and flourished for many years. The St. James congregation of the African Methodist Episcopal Church served as the black community's social and religious foundation. Blacks in Helena found success in nearly every occupation and the newspapers devoted numerous column inches to bringing to public attention the achievements of its readership.

"The state of Montana," reads *The Colored Citizen*'s inaugural issue, "has just right to feel proud of its twenty-five hundred colored citizens found in every county of this fair and prosperous commonwealth. They are to a man wealth producers. They are of the brawn that have unfettered and exposed to the sunshine of our unsurpassed clime the treasured wealth of ages..." J.P. Ball, Jr., editor and manager of *The Colored Citizen*, and his financial backers (purported to be white politicians eager to claim victory in the famed Helena-Anaconda capital-city contest) believed that Montana's black voting populous was large enough to significantly sway the vote for Helena as Montana's capital city. Ball hoped the black voters to which he directed his paper would obstruct the Anaconda Company's "iron claw of corporate infernalism which has always crushed out the black man from every factory and workshop." In an article entitled "Anaconda Draws the Color Line," Ball explained how his staff was thwarted in an attempt to exchange information and articles with the *Anaconda Standard*. Stating that this was "evidently a case of colorphobia," Ball urged his readers to "vote or work against Anaconda," adding, "our paper must be respected."

The Colored Citizen met its end when its purported primary objective was met. Helena became the capital city and the town's black community lost an eloquent spokesperson.

This role would be assumed again in 1906 by Joseph B. Bass, a social and political activist from Topeka, Kansas, who arrived in Helena and soon began publishing the *Montana*

Plaindealer. The *Plaindealer*'s first issue appeared on March 6, 1906, promising to "advocate the principles of Peace, Prosperity and Union...stand up for the right and denounce the wrong," and "at no time stir up strife but rather to pour oil on troubled waters." Like *The Colored Citizen*, the *Plaindealer* embraced most tenets of the Republican party. But Bass claimed that in the *Plaindealer* "politics shall always be subordinate to the interests and welfare of our people," adding that while the paper would take a definite stand on political issues, it would also continually strive to benefit its black readership.

Bass quickly immersed himself and the paper in volatile local political issues. In June 1906, city officials acted to close the Zanzibar Saloon, a predominantly black establishment. The *Helena Daily Independent* had called the saloon "the vilest, the most insolent, the most degenerate and the most anomalous warren of salacity and sin that Montana ever knew..." Bass retorted with headlines claiming "HELENA IS OPEN! GAMBLING RUNNING FULL BLAST!" The *Plaindealer* followed these attention-grabbers with a series of reports detailing gambling violations throughout Helena, and chastised city officials who did nothing to stop them. Before long, the Zanzibar reopened under another name.

Bass and his publication became heavily involved in local elections. As a reward for his partisan endeavors, the state Republican caucus had proposed that Bass be appointed as a staff person for the upcoming legislative session. When the appointment failed to come through, Bass exhorted, "The Republicans have said by their actions...'You may vote for us; you may take off your coats and work for us; but when it comes to emoluments of office, *we have none of that for you*'."

The Republican Party again disillusioned Bass when in 1909 a Republican-controlled state Senate passed a bill prohibiting intermarriage between whites, blacks and Asians. Bass commented in the *Plaindealer* that the bill's passage in the Senate was a "keen disappointment to our people, and what a surprise when the Republicans dealt the blow; going squarely back on one of the planks of their platform in the last campaign." After the Democratic House passed the measure in a 29-25 vote, an editorial appearing in the *Plaindealer* lamented, "Montana has joined the Jim Crow Colony alongside of Mississippi, South Carolina, Texas and Arkansas. God help us!"

Shortly after this defeat, the *Plaindealer* suffered a series of financial setbacks, culminating in its demise with its September 8, 1911, issue. *The Colored Citizen* and the *Montana Plaindealer* not only served as informative, eloquent and articulate voices for Helena's black citizens, they provide us today with a firsthand glimpse into the lives of a population too often overlooked in the annals of Western history.

HELENA
PLACES

Rebirth of a City

BY Harriett C.
Meloy

The "old" Queen City, in the 1890s.

A still controversial era in Helena's history began in the
late 1960s and lasted through the 1970s. During those years,
the character of our city was changed forever. This time span
was known by Urban Renewal.

Narrating the intricacies of Helena's '60s to '70s renewal is
a challenge for a sociologist, architect or urban planner. This
author is none of these. Even so, a brief foray into the past
may answer newcomers' questions about the city's history, and

remind old-timers what they've almost forgotten about how and why Helena's downtown was permanently altered.

Historians hasten to remind readers up front that an urban renewal in Helena took its first steps more than a century ago as a result of natural and social events. Disastrous fires in 1869, 1871, 1874 and 1879 inflicted millions of dollars of damage on businesses in the Gulch and city officials recommended urban improvement. One of the first improvements was the addition of firefighting equipment and the installation of more cisterns. In the rebuilding that followed each of these conflagrations, brick and stone replaced wooden structures lost by fire. One of these early brick buildings was the Merchants Bank, later the Union Bank, which was built in 1889 on the northwest corner of Last Chance Gulch and Edwards, just south of the present Park Plaza. This bank, designed with fire prevention in mind, was constructed with a double wall in the middle to prevent spread of fire between the two ends of the structure. It never did succumb to fire, but was one of the substantial buildings razed by Urban Renewal in the early 1970s.

Fligelman's store, and the Gold Block, burned in 1928, were rebuilt immediately to fill in the vacant area and make the upper end of Last Chance Gulch whole again.

Other fires burned Broadwater's Montana National Bank on Main and Edwards in January 1944, the Harvey Hotel on Main Street in 1967, the Grandon Hotel on Sixth and Warren in 1968, the Horsky Building in 1980, and the Denver Block in 1981. (Centennial Park replaced the Horsky building, and the Workers' Compensation parking structure arose in the space left by the burned Denver Block.) Another calamity befell the city in October, 1935, when a major earthquake struck. Few buildings were utterly destroyed, but in the aftermath many decorative appurtenances, steeples and towers—Victorian characteristics—were removed to guarantee safety. Helena's look and character were decisively changing.

More profoundly altering than fire and earthquake was the automobile's influence on the city. During the 1940s businesses moved out to the fringes of town; these stores and firms boasted plenty of parking space in comparison to little or none on Last Chance Gulch. Downtown gradually lost its heart as

Above: The Old Brewery.
Right: A common site
during the Urban
Renewal years.

rents and building maintenance declined, leaving the historic city center run down and abandoned.

In the mid-1960s Helena's business people and city officials agonized over how to save the central city. They recognized that revitalizing the city depended on a large infusion of capital. Then, in 1967, Mayor Darryl Lee and other city officials, together with the private group, Helena First, Inc., applied for Model Cities designation from the federal government, hoping that it would result in receipt of thousands of dollars for Helena. They were successful in garnering more than $40 million for three programs: The Model Cities Project, Urban Renewal, and Community Block Grants.

Model Cities, the introductory program, required huge citizen participation with many committees, boards and neighborhood councils meeting to design a comprehensive plan. One *Independent Record* reporter commented that the "requirements for citizen participation gave the local community its biggest dose of democracy since the gold seekers in Last Chance Gulch agreed to share their campfire." Neighborhood councils elected outreach workers to serve as liaison agents with residents; two of these aides were Robert Richeson and Richard Spurzem.

Judith Carlson wrote the first Model City proposal, and became its director. When she left in 1973 for another position, she gave high marks to the city, saying, "Widespread citizen participation in many phases of governmental decision-making is now city policy." Carlson congratulated Helenans for their willing involvement in the program: "We have demonstrated that, given the opportunity, citizens will share in formulating city goals and activities."

Participation, however praiseworthy, did not guarantee consensus about changes the program would make in historic downtown Helena. There were, of course, enthusiastic advocates. Charles J. "Si" Seifert, speaking in a debate over the proposed Main Street pedestrian mall said, "We are about to open the most exciting downtown in Montana." But others were deeply concerned that acceptance of Model Cities funds might mean that all structures in the zone would have to be brought up to federal specifications or sold to the Urban Renewal program to bring them up to code or demolish them.

Larry Gallagher, who became Urban Renewal director in 1972, was responsible for many of the difficult decisions mandated by the program such as destruction of the Monticello apartments, the Brewery Theater on West Main, and the Helena apartments on Grand Street. One of the most controversial demolitions was that of the Brewery Theater.

In all, says archivist Christian Frazza, who recently prepared an Urban Renewal photo exhibit, "Over 230 structures were demolished, including 71 commercial buildings and 123 residences." Many of these structures defined the Helena historic district. Two of the most notable buildings, the Marlow Theater and the Union Bank stood in the way of a planned extension of Broadway to Park Avenue, as well as took up

Early Urban Renewal Model.   DAVE SHORS/INDEPENDENT RECORD

spaces designated for parking lots. An additional problem was that no one came forward and offered to bring the buildings up to federal code to save them. As a result—and to the dismay of local citizens—the Marlow Theater and the Union Bank came down.

While the effect of Urban Renewal on the central historic downtown area was contested, there was consensus about changes on South Main. Among buildings erected on South Main was the new federal building arising where the AA Garage once stood; a new architecturally attractive public library was built; and the Neighborhood Center emerged just south of the library. Below the rehabilitated, historic "Bluestone Building," apartments were constructed to house low-income senior citizens. Very little criticism was heard about the architectural design of these buildings, which may indicate that their appearance was more acceptable than the displaced structures.

Despite Si Seifert's early optimism about Helenans' acceptance of a downtown mall, many citizens still express doubts concerning the removal of automobiles from Main Street, and from year to year someone seriously suggests bringing two-way traffic back to Last Chance Gulch.

A group of Helena's well-established businesses such as Fligelman's (which later became MacDonald's), J.C. Penney's, Parchen's Drug and a number offices remained on the downtown mall, stressing need for parking—a matter that Helena officials and businessmen knew must be resolved. To alleviate the concern, a 450-car city-owned parking structure, corner of Park and Sixth, was opened in October 1976.

Helena's city leaders and residents were certain that plans for renewal of their city were confirmed by the 1980s. The influence of federal programs, Model Cities and Community Block Grant development along with Urban Renewal was the guiding force that actually contributed to change. Proponents of the federal programs were grateful for the influx of federal money. But many Helena citizens worried about the influence of the federal government not understanding the needs of the capital city, or dictating control of Helena's destiny. A concern about historic preservation of business buildings in Last Chance Gulch was a divisive matter—and continues today when demolition of the Marlow Theater is mentioned.

Because of the federal programs, Helena's inner core was changed and, most people believed, for the better. The downtown mall, the new buildings, preservation of the old buildings, can be attributed to the efforts of courageous Helena people who realized we must always preserve the pioneer spirit of change to sustain this city as one of the most desirable places to live in Montana and in the U.S.A.

GOD'S ACRE

BY CHERE JIUSTO

We are only a breath in the tempest of time
We seek, and the centuries laugh.
We are only faint shadows in the infinite gloom
With a breeze for an epitaph.

On March 7, 1865, Dr. L. Rodney Pococke claimed the dubious honor of being the first person to die in the Last Chance mining camp. In the custom of the day, he was probably taken to a site a short distance out of town, and interred. Over time, others followed Dr. Pococke into the next world, and a 10-acre site of open land along the Benton Road became the burying place for the town.

Early on, the cemetery was plotted in classic Victorian style, with a circle at the center and over 1,200 burial plots arranged in neat, square rows. The northeast section was reserved for members of the Masonic Lodge. The earliest markers remaining date to 1867. In all, there are over 800 graves from before 1880.

Over the years, the cemetery carried various names—God's Acre, Greenwood Cemetery and the Helena Cemetery.

Influential businessman Charles A. Broadwater acquired the cemetery property in 1881, and exchanged it with Lewis and Clark County for other land. The county turned management responsibilities over to the Benton Avenue Cemetery Association in 1922. In 1930, the ornate iron fence and gates were added "in memory of Major James R. Boyce and other Pioneers." But over the years that followed, the Benton Avenue Cemetery was abandoned.

For over four decades, weeds grew high and "God's acre" became a dump for every kind of refuse: cans, bottles, mattresses, wheels, lumber and other trash.

Then, in 1966, a local woman named Lucy Baker launched a crusade to restore the cemetery. A secretary who worked at the state capitol, Lucy drove up Benton Avenue daily en route to work. Convinced that the beleaguered cemetery deserved better treatment, she issued a challenge to the women of Helena to come out and help clean out the property.

Once the debris was cleared away, Lucy Baker and others examined headstones and searched

The Benton Avenue Cemetery.

through old records to compile a list of those buried in Benton Avenue Cemetery. Many of Helena's earliest residents—miners and merchants, pioneers and politicians—were laid to rest here.

Wandering through the cemetery you can still find such names as John Kinna, a vigilante and first mayor of Helena; Valentine Priest, who built the Priest Pass road with the help of a hundred Chinese workmen; Cyrus S. Ingersoll, Helena's "gold rush doctor" and his wife, Calista Gay, mining camp midwife who delivered the babies of Helena; Louis Reeder, the Pennsylvania stonemason who built Reeder's Alley; Michael Reinig, John R. Sanford, S.H. Crounse, John Horsky, Joseph Farrow, early merchants in the bustling queen city.

There are those that tug at your heart. A child's grave marked by a small straw hat and shoes in an empty chair. Two babies from one family laid near one another. Children and adults who succumbed to a scarlet fever epidemic of 1877.

And perhaps most moving, the markers where time has worn away the names. Stone markers where you can trace inscriptions with your finger but the letters can no longer be read. Bare wooden markers where a loved one was buried but is now long forgotten. Markers broken off at the base and desecrated by someone unknown.

At Benton Avenue Cemetery, many stories of our past are kept. The hopes, the dreams, the pride and the heartache of life in early-day Helena. Visit there some quiet day, and listen hard if the breezes are blowing.

THE HELENA DEPOT DISTRICT

BY HARRIETT C. MELOY

On June 12, 1883, in a grassy pasture at the northeast corner of Helena, the noisy Winston Brothers construction train pulled to a stop. There a year or two later the N.P. depot was built. This first depot still exists at 1330 E. Lyndale although now it looks more like the church it later became.

In 1904, the Northern Pacific Railroad Company's annual report announced that a new depot would be built in Helena to provide more space for a passenger waiting room, a larger baggage and express room, and a larger restaurant (the N.P. Beanery was always a favorite place to eat even for people who were not using the railway.) This stately building, at the east end of Helena Avenue, houses the Montana Rail Link offices today.

While Helena's overall population expanded somewhat during the late 1880s and into the turn of the century, population growth in the depot district was phenomenal. Most arrived to work on the railroad. It took a large number of railroad workers to service the four transcontinental trains per day as well as the twenty-two feeder lines that supplied transportation to all the bustling gold and silver camps in Helena's neighborhood—Wickes, Rimini, Marysville, Elkhorn and Confederate Gulch, to name a few.

The district's ethnic blend made a colorful addition to Helena's more sedate main-street society. Irish, French, German, Scandinavian, Finlander, Icelander, English, Italian, Japanese and Chinese arrived with the railroad. According to J. Einar

Larson, who provided the information contained herein, the area at one time was known as the "Bloody Sixth" (referring to its political identity as the Sixth Ward) because it was populated by a number of Irish who were reputed to have hot tempers. Thus, "It was as easy to pick a bloody fight as it was to say 'good morning, Pat'."

Employment with the railroad called for countless skills. Engineers, firemen, brakemen, conductors, section crews, engine repairmen, switchmen, baggage haulers, expressmen, cooks and waiters, freight handlers, ice crews, yard masters, superintendent, round-house foreman, mechanics, boilermakers, fire cleaners, call boys and mail-car workers were job descriptions of a large number of the Sixth Ward citizens.

Early on, wages were low. A man was paid $1.40 for ten hours of work on the section, and $1.75 on the coal dock shoveling coal ten hours a day. Overalls cost 50 cents and a good suit $12.50. A large glass of Kessler beer sold for 5 cents. Living was cheap too, Larson reports. "For a single man's board and room the cost was $20.00 a month. Two pounds of roundsteak sold for 25 cents and four pounds of boiling beef—25 cents. Whole or half a beef sold for 4 cents per pound—wholesale. Whole dressed hogs were 7 and a half cents per pound. Liver was free. Eggs cost customers $1.00 a dozen at Christmas time, but the grocer gave customers a dozen oranges or apples when they paid their bill. The butcher bought drinks."

The butcher, H. Walter Larson, immigrated to the U.S. from Sweden in 1902, traveling directly to Helena where an aunt and uncle provided a home for him. He opened a meat market close to the railroad station, but moved across the street to 1413 Helena Avenue. In 1913 that became the home of the Montana Meat Company, which at first was a retail and grocery business but later expanded into a "full scale packing plant selling all cuts of beef, veal and pork and curing hams, bacon and sausage." He became one of the most prominent members of the Sixth Ward community.

In fact, this district produced many prominent Helenans. One was Lewis O. Brackman of Brackman's Grocery Stores. Another was William D. (Bud) Ferrat, reputedly a big-league baseball player in his youth, who owned a favorite eating and

The original depot building, with the Grand Pacific Hotel to its immediate left, 1885.

drinking business always referred to as "Ferrat's." When beer became legal, Ferrat's catered to customers in automobiles who parked in front of the restaurant. The Schneider family, including Peg Schneider Condon who still lives in the original depot building, developed a rug factory in that same building. Alice Israel and Theo Smith were two of the most popular teachers in Bryant School. And three Helena mayors lived for a time in the Sixth Ward: Jack Haytin, Russ Ritter (whose father owned a drug store on Helena Avenue) and Kathleen Ramey, who was also a popular high school teacher.

Nearness to the railroad station and freight office stimulated business growth not only along Helena Avenue but throughout the depot district. Firms that built warehouses or branch offices in the Sixth Ward bore names of some of Helena's eminent citizens—Goldberg Hide and Fur, H. Earl Clack Company, Schaeffer Wholesale Grocery, Brown Brothers Lumber Company, Eck Mobile Oil and Gas, Curtin and Dehler, Holter Warehouse, Crago Warehouse and Storage, Barnett Iron Works, T.C. Power Storage, Caird Engineering and others. Renovated almost beyond recognition, on Boulder Avenue, the National Biscuit Company building is a reminder of one of the Helena's largest industries.

When automobiles and automated locomotives arrived on the scene, the Sixth Ward community changed drastically. Because few railroaders were needed, most workers went into other fields of employment, some retired, others left the state. A few landmarks survived. The Larson Block, which at one time housed the Montana Meat Company, Ferrat's, Brackman's store, the Farmers and Mechanic State Bank, a barber shop and saloon, is still maintained on Helena Avenue.

What's gone, what remains?

More than a hundred years since the first N.P. train arrived in Helena, the Sixth Ward still has a distinctive flavor that sets it apart from any other Helena neighborhood. Gone are the sounds of words spoken in foreign tongues; gone are the lines of passengers waiting to board one of the several trains a day; gone is the bustle of wagons, horses and trucks on Helena Avenue. But much of the early architecture is still in evidence. The homes of railroaders still stand along what is now Phoenix Avenue, including the railroad superintendent's home on the south side of the street toward the tracks. The handsome railroad station itself is a reminder of the past. Remnants of the Caird Engineering company (the pattern house that is now a coffee shop) tell another story of their own. The early St. Mary's Catholic Church, turned Head Start headquarters, is now a church again on Roberts. Because of the appearance of the area and the fact that children and grandchildren of early Sixth Ward residents still live in family homes along the quiet streets, it's fairly certain that the special quality of the area will remain intact into the future—perhaps another hundred years.

A Toast to Hale Reservoir

BY CHERE JIUSTO

Water in Helena has long been a precious commodity. In the Last Chance mining camp, water was prized more for mining than for drinking. Down in the diggings, gold panning and sluicing required water, and lots of it, to wash away soil and gravel, leaving only flakes and nuggets of yellow metal in the goldpans.

The first water directed into Helena was for mining, via the Yaw Yaw ditch of 1865. Snaking in from the west around the base of Mount Helena, it delivered water from Ten Mile Creek to the mines.

Through the late 19th century, other water systems were built around town, all private ventures. One water developer was Robert S. Hale, a native of Kentucky, druggist and gold rush entrepreneur. Hale came to Helena in 1865 via Virginia City, purchased mining claims here and opened a drug store in Last Chance Gulch.

In 1869, Hale joined with several capitalists to organize the Park Ditch Company, which harnessed water for mining from Park Lake, 20 miles southwest of Helena. Hale soon bought out his partners in the Park Ditch Company, and used it to mine his claims. Heavily invested in the Helena gold fields, he owned most of the mining claims between the Helena city limits and the head of Grizzly Gulch, along with numerous claims in Dry Gulch and Oro Fino Gulch.

The old Hale Reservoir continues to deliver sweet, clear water.

As the Last Chance placer mines played out and the dust settled in the mining camp, owners sold their water rights to quench the thirst of growing Helena. During the latter 1800s, four systems were developed for local drinking water. R.S. Hale built the Hale water system during the 1880s, harnessing underground water from springs in Oro Fino Gulch. From there, water was carried along the southern contours of the gulch, a route we know as the Water Line Trail, and collected in a reservoir overlooking downtown and Helena's original neighborhood.

The Hale Reservoir was constructed of locally quarried stone atop Rodney Ridge by Frank Jezick, a Croatian stonecutter and mason. A tradesman of great skill, Jezick also worked on such imposing stone buildings as the Helena High School (demolished in the 1970s) and his own home below the reservoir on Clancy Street.

For over 100 years now, the old Hale Reservoir has delivered sweet, clear water to the southern portions of Helena. Recently, a second Hale reservoir was built higher up the ridge.

It ties into the historic Hale system, adding 200,000 gallons of capacity, to improve pressure and fire protection in this early neighborhood.

But the new reservoir will never be the work of art that old Hale Reservoir is. It is not formed of stone carved from the hillsides of Helena, laid carefully by hand to last for centuries. That new reservoir is simply an enormous tank, with no heart and no soul. It was painted to blend with the environment, and most of us will try to ignore it. We won't walk up to it and admire it, knock on the old wooden doors, and marvel at the skill it took to build it.

So, a tribute to the old Hale Reservoir. Fill your glasses with that sweet spring water and drink a toast in memory of R.S. Hale, Frank Jezick and all those other builders of long ago Helena. They just don't build them like they used to.

LeGrande Cannon Boulevard

BY HARRIETT C.
MELOY

The naming of Helena's streets seems to have been as haphazard as their many curves and turns. Some streets, of course, have reasoned titles, such as those bearing numbers or the names of pioneers. But, what about LeGrande Cannon Boulevard that circles Mount Helena's north side? It has aroused curiosity and inquiry for almost a century.

First, let's clear up the street's persistent misnomers. The proper name is not the "Grand Boulevard," which Helenans called the road early in the 20th century. Nor is it "Grand Canyon" or "Le Grande Canyon" boulevard, titles that many use today. It was named LeGrande Cannon in 1906, after the son of prominent Helenan, Charles W. Cannon.

We've traced the antecedents of the Helena Cannon family to the 17th century. In 1692, after the Edict of Nantes was revoked, Jan Cannon was one of many who left France to escape religious persecution and immigrated to America. Several generations later, in 1863, Charles W. Cannon migrated with his brother Henry to Helena in search of a fortune.

They did not find gold, but Charles and Henry began a grocery business with provisions brought from home. Excellent merchandisers, the two young men became successful enough to branch off into other businesses. Together they purchased a 16,000-acre sheep ranch in Cascade County, and Henry developed their woolgrowing business into the largest in the region. In 1907, he sold the ranch to Henry Sieben.

In 1882, while still tending the prosperous grocery business, Charles turned his attention to real estate and mining. By 1889, his recorded wealth was listed as $176,570, a little less than Hauser's $193,790, and a little more than A.M. Holter's $120,620.

Two years later, Charles Cannon was considered "the largest individual owner of property on which taxes are levied in this state." He put his income to work by investing with Col. Charles Broadwater in gas, electric and street railway systems in Helena.

A number of years earlier, in 1868, Charles Cannon and Catherine Martine, originally of New York City, were married in Dubuque, Iowa. Upon returning to Helena, the Cannons moved into their beautiful frame home on the corner of Ewing and Broadway. Distinguished by its high pitched roof and narrow floor-to-ceiling windows, this early Helena mansion has been preserved in its unique style.

In this house, a daughter, Bernice Martinique, was born to the Cannons in 1869. It was she who, as a small child, lighted the first gas fixture in the city. Always fragile, she became seriously ill after she left Helena to attend school on Long Island. At the age of 18, she died in her mother's arms in the home where she was born.

Their only other child, William LeGrande Cannon, was born in 1880. He was eight years of age when his sister died. At the behest of his father, a major stockholder, he pounded the first spike into the tracks when Helena's street railways were launched in 1886. His life of privilege wasn't entirely immune to danger. The *Helena Daily Herald,* April 25, 1890, reported that "two roughly clad men" attempted to assault the young man late at night when he returned from the opera and began to unlock the door of his house. One man "caught Will by the throat," but young Cannon jerked away and blew a whistle summoning his father, who opened the door and threatened to shoot the intruders. Evidently, the men intended to rob the Cannons, but were interrupted by the son appearing, and his bravery.

William LeGrande was educated in Helena as a child, but since he later meant to go to the best schools in the world, he was sent to St. Paul's Episcopal School in Concord, New Hampshire.

From there he traveled to France and Germany where he attended schools with Charles and William Clark, sons of Senator

Above: Helena's scenic LeGrande Cannon Boulevard.
Top left: Charles W. Cannon.
Top right: William LeGrande Cannon.

W.A. Clark. Described always in the most felicitous terms, the Cannon son was said to be a young man of extraordinary talent and intelligence, as well as being handsome and personable.

William LeGrande fell victim to tuberculosis. His health deteriorated during his travels, and on February 9, 1903, he died, leaving his grief-stricken father and mother without an heir.

Bereft of all that was near and dear to them, the anguished parents began searching for a lasting memorial to their son. An idea came their way on January 6, 1906, when Professor Henry Turner Bailey, a noted landscape artist, visited Helena to lecture on beautifying the Territorial Capital. Dr. Bailey advocated constructing a road along the abandoned Chessman reservoir ditch, which had been dug around Mount Helena's base in the early days of placer mining to carry the waters of Ten Mile into Last Chance and Dry gulches. The Helena Improvement Society seized upon this suggestion because it promised to become what one Helena journalist described as "an ideal roadway."

Another *Helena Independent* reporter intoned the roadway's praises: "Did you ever appreciate the fact that high above the dust and monotony of the valley, skirting the margin of the forest park, sheltered from the winds and following the natural inundations of the mountains, the driveway offers scenic possibilities unparalleled in all America?"

After looking over the prospective route, an eminent group waxed "loud in their praises of the grandeur the view afforded." The group included railway builder James J. Hill, president of the Northern Pacific Railway, Howard Elliot, partner of J.P. Morgan, Charles Steele, and president of the First National Bank of New York, George F. Baker.

Imbued with the enthusiasm of the Helena community and the distinguished visitors, Charles and Catherine Cannon gave $5,000 to Helena officials for construction of the boulevard within the city limits, and asked that the road be named for their son. And so LeGrande Cannon Boulevard was constructed.

The road ended at the Broadwater Natatorium, probably under the guidance of Charles Broadwater.

Helena citizens young and old have enjoyed the thoroughfare for over a hundred years to do any number of things—to jog, to walk the dog, to watch the moon rise, to…

Lenox, Exclusive East-Side Subdivision

❦

BY HARRIETT C. MELOY

Helena's Victorian architecture gained an immense boost during the final years of the 19th century when several farsighted investors discovered that Montana's capitol would be built on five acres of land a mile east of the city's center. This site offered much, "with the background of hills an aesthetic advantage, and its location on the electric rail line a practical consideration."

The Victorian mansion era in Helena ended with the 1893 Silver Panic. This home is at 1735 Jerome.

Even before the ink was dry on the capitol-site deed, Peter Winne was laying out a subdivision on a "plateau" to the southeast of that site. His plan was to build homes to rival any of the fine mansions on the west side or in the competing Kenwood addition. Winne, recently from Denver, and six other investors became the Denver Land Investment Company. They hired realtors Wallace and Thornburgh to promote a spring land-sale in 1890. Half-page newspaper ads beckoned prospective buyers to the east side; one read "'Westward the tide of Empire' may be true enough of the whole country, but in Helena EASTWARD the tide of building for residence has surely turned."

The realtors took the name Lenox for their subdivision. According to Jean Baucus in *Helena, Her Story,* Vol. II, page 21, the name Lenox came from the fashionable area of New York City by the same name.

Financier Theodore H. Kleinschmidt was one of the first to invest. In 1892, he built a home at 1823 Highland. His Victorian mansion became the subdivision's centerpiece, which to this day is declared to be one of the best examples of Queen Anne Victorian architecture in the region.

Kleinschmidt was a three-time Helena mayor, a great contributor to the community's Presbyterian Church, and owner of at least 1,000 acres of land in Lewis and Clark County. As a notable entrepreneur, he intended the mansion as another investment. However, financial reversals caused by the 1893 Silver Panic ordained that Kleinschmidt abandon his hopes to sell the home for a profit, and instead he moved his family into the mansion. He lived there for the rest of his life. Janet Sperry is now the proud owner of the T.H. Kleinschmidt house.

The same year that Kleinschmidt built his home, Jack V. Jerome also built a mansion in the Queen Anne style, a block west, at 1721 Highland. The current owner of this home, Lewis Brackman, speculates about Jack Jerome's origins. Jerome's middle name was Vanderbilt; his last name was the same as Winston Churchill's American mother, Jenny Jerome, who was also the daughter of financier Leonard Jerome of New York City. Although his names may be coincidental, perhaps Jack Jerome was descended from these New York scions. His career in banking, which began in 1883-84 (he was listed in the Helena City Directory as a First National Bank bookkeeper), may lend credence to the idea that he was connected to New York's financial sphere.

We know for certain that Jack Jerome was hospitable and fun loving. When the new streetcar line to Lenox opened in early January 1892, he hosted a party "providing a fine collation [light meal] and champagne" to partygoers who were delivered to his home in two horsedrawn cars. He died in 1897, no doubt in the East, since his obituary does not appear in Helena newspapers.

On a nearby street named after the popular Jerome, Frank Michael Meyendorff built the handsome home at 1815 Jerome Place, in 1891, but he lived in the mansion only a short time. The son of a Polish count, Meyendorff was banished from Poland to Siberia for taking up arms against Russia during a Polish independence bid. Through the influence of his father, he came to the U.S. and earned an engineering degree at the University of Michigan. He arrived in Helena during the 1870s to design and build the United States Assay Building, which still stands today on Broadway.

Meyendorff lived in his Lenox mansion for approximately two years; it's uncertain just why he left. He did remain in Helena, a popular figure in the community's social circles, until 1896 when he left for federal government employment to expose land frauds in Utah and Colorado. His death in 1908 was reported from Portland, Oregon.

Meyendorff's Jerome Place home was "restored" a number of times, but the essential quality of Queen Anne architecture—its solid oak woodwork, distinctive wrap-around porches, granite stonework, shingled façade and small-paned windows—remains, a credit to its original builder.

The precise number of early Lenox homes was variously reported. Perhaps 20 mansions were built; of these at least 15 still exist. Fire destroyed several homes, possibly before 1910.

As one looks at this historic subdivision, a question arises: Why were the majority of mansions constructed on Winne, Jerome and Highland in a descending row—one in front of the other down the hill—rather than in an east-west alignment?

One good answer is that a deep ravine ran north and south in the Corbin Addition just to the west of 1733 Winne, 1721 Jerome Place and 1721 Highland. (This ravine served as the city garbage dump until it was filled shortly after the capitol was built.)

Most of the homes in the Lenox subdivision were continuously inhabited during the 20th century, yet the majority of renters or purchasers remained for only a few years at a time. This provides for an interesting contrast to most of Helena's west-side mansions, in which one family lived for decades, or even for a lifetime.

Lenox mansions did rival in appearance and richness a num-

Another Lenox delight, at 1735 Highland.

ber of the fine west-side homes. But after the 1893 Panic, building in the new east-side subdivision ceased. The area was never again found desirable for large expensive residences, even after the capitol was built. The Victorian mansion era in Helena had ended.

Though Lenox never lived up to its originators' plans for an exclusive suburb, it did prosper in the 1950s and '60s, when Helenans filled in the area with low ranch-style houses and bungalows. Amidst these post-war era homes, the Victorian mansions of the early subdivision still stand out, reminders of Helena's rich past.

Lime Kilns Crucial in Helena's Development

BY JON AXLINE

Helena is certainly blessed with all material neces-
sary for building purposes. Stone quarries consisting
of granite, slate, and other rock; limestone in endless
quantities; and pine lumber in great abundance—all
within a few miles of the city.
                    Helena Weekly Independent, *1884*

Like castle towers, the lime kilns stand sentinel at the junction of Oro Fino and Grizzly gulches. The kilns played a significant role in the development of Helena in the late 19th century. The product derived from them was used to make mortar,
plaster and stucco—the stuff that holds many of our old buildings together. How the kilns operated and who owned them
provide a fascinating insight into Helena's early construction
industry.

Limestone is made from the skeletons of countless sea crea-
tures that, when compacted and fused, form an excellent building material. Helena is conveniently located near an extensive
limestone outcrop that stretches between Ten Mile and Prickly Pear creeks. The first residents of Last Chance Gulch took
advantage of the limestone deposits shortly after the camp was
established in 1864. But it was not until the catastrophic fires
of the 1870s that Helena's business and home owners were
intimidated into building more substantial structures of stone

and brick; lime production boomed as a result. With this momentous change in the use of building material, the very fabric and appearance of the Queen City were transformed. Several companies quickly formed to take advantage of the huge demand for lime in the 1870s and early 1880s.

Lime kiln sites usually consisted of the limestone quarry, the kiln and an attached cooling shed. The kilns on Grizzly Gulch are located immediately below the cliffs that supplied the limestone. At some operations the limestone was literally rolled down the hill to the kilns. From there, it was broken up and fed into the top of the structure. Fire holes on each side of the kiln were fired with wood to heat the limestone to a temperature of 1,648° Fahrenheit. After baking for about 8 hours, the lime chunks inside the kiln would collapse, dropping the material into the brick-lined clean-up hole in the front of the structure. From there, it would be pulled into the cooling shed, stacked and transported to an area where it would later be slaked with water. Slaking reduced the lime into a fine powder that would be used to manufacture cement, mortar and plaster. Running day and night, each kiln produced about three tons of lime every 24 hours.

Irish immigrant Joseph O'Neill constructed the first lime kiln on Grizzly Gulch in the early 1870s. O'Neill arrived in Helena in early 1865 and quickly learned to "mine the miners" once he found all the profitable mining claims taken up. The first lime kiln O'Neill constructed is the second structure from the south on Grizzly Gulch; he had built a second kiln by 1884. Ironically for O'Neill, the *Helena Weekly Independent* reported in June 1884 that a rich pocket of gold quartz was discovered during excavation of the second structure's foundation. The expansion of O'Neill's operations coincided with the building boom Helena was then experiencing. The *Weekly Independent* stated that other kilns were then being constructed in nearby Lime Kiln Gulch and at a site east of Helena. The reporter also claimed that the remains of older kilns were readily apparent in the hills surrounding the gulch.

O'Neill built two additional lime kilns before he sold the operation in the late 1890s to James Kervin, who, in turn, sold them to a former O'Neill employee, James McKelvey. Many of

Running day and night, each kiln produced about three tons of lime every 24 hours.

the old homes on West Main Street housed lime-kiln workers. The lime kilns continued to thrive until the early 1900s when competition from a company in Elliston forced the business to close. Because the Elliston kilns were located closer to the Northern Pacific Railroad tracks they were able to ship their product more cheaply to points throughout Montana. The McKelveys briefly reopened the Grizzly Gulch kilns in the 1930s, possibly to provide lime for exterior stuccoing. The boom, however, proved to be short-lived and the kilns were shut down permanently after the 1935 earthquakes.

One of the most intact lime-kiln complexes in the Helena area is up a gulch just off Gold Rush Avenue on the upper east side. Little is known of the operation other than a short mention in the *Lenox Lance*, a neighborhood newsletter printed by the first residents of the Lenox subdivision. The May 1903 edition stated, "The picnic season opened...when the Lenox School and its guests went on a day's outing in the hills near

Smither's lime kiln." The lime produced in this structure was likely used for mortar and plaster of the mansions gracing the swanky neighborhood.

The lime kiln is located a short distance up a narrow gulch that empties onto Gold Rush Avenue. The quarry is located on the hillside above the kiln and cooling shed. There is also a small leveled off space just above the kiln where some kind of shack was once situated. On the trail up to the kiln, you can also see where a load of lime was accidentally dumped on the ground. The lime kiln was probably used for a relatively short time, but has since made a permanent mark on the preadolescent social history of the area. In the years before the area was subdivided, the kiln was scene of many make-believe wars between the neighborhood kids living just above St. Peters Hospital. We had no idea what the kiln was or why it was there.

The lime kilns played a crucial role in the development of Helena in the late 19th century. The material produced in them is literally the glue that holds many of our historic buildings together. The manufacture of lime was also an important part of the city's economic well-being since it was sold to other communities throughout the state. Although the future of the lime kiln off Gold Rush Avenue is clouded because of population pressures in the South Hills, those located on Grizzly Gulch will be listed on the National Register of Historic Places in 1996; they will continue to stand watch on West Main Street.

Marysville: Hub of Commerce

BY HARRIETT C. MELOY

Marysville, a gem of a mining village on the eastern edge of the Continental Divide, traces its roots to a defining event in Ireland's history over a century and a half ago, The Great Potato Famine. With the destruction of Ireland's main subsistence crop, thousands of Irish people emigrated to this country for work and food. One emigrant, Thomas Cruse, came to Montana by way of New York and Sutter's Mill.

In 1969, Cruse arrived in Trinity Gulch after a brief stay in Helena. He met William Brown, who befriended the down-and-out Irishman and grubstaked him through the winter, offering work at his placer digs. Cruse, curious about a high-grade ore that kept sticking to his sluice pan, decided to locate its source. His inquisitiveness paid off. In 1868, Cruse located a body of quartz on the mountain south of present-day Marysville, and several years later he found the mother lode. Always a taciturn individual, Cruse quietly went to the courthouse in Helena and claimed the mine, which, according to some reports, belonged to George Detweiler, a member of the first territorial legislature. Detweiler did not challenge Cruse's action. Cruse named the mine Drumlummon after his home parish.

Meanwhile other mines were developed in the area, including Nate Vestal's Penobscot and Snow Drift. More miners arrived, Cornish and Irish, lured by the hope of work and, better still, wealth. One of the first families to arrive was Cornish,

The Lightbody House, circa 1890.

made up of Mary and Sam Ralston and their eleven children. Mary was not only caretaker and nurse of her own brood, but drew the entire community into her motherly embrace. Tommy Cruse was so impressed by her that he named the town in Mary's honor.

As swamps were cleared and more Drumlummon ore mined, Cruse realized he could no longer continue to work his five-stamp mill without more capital and equipment. Wishing to realize the full value of the mine, but with no desire to acquire partners, he sold the claim to an English syndicate, retaining rights to a large portion of the royalties. When the English arrived, the future of Marysville was assured as a hub of commerce, communication and transportation.

After selling his mine, Thomas Cruse moved to Helena, built a fine home, established a bank and married Margaret Mary Carter, the sister of delegate to Congress Thomas Carter. Margaret, a number of years younger than her husband, taught Tommy the rudiments of reading and writing. W.W. DeLacy, in chronicling 1886 Helena events, reported that Cruse always walked several steps behind his wife on their way to church. Possibly this was Cruse's way of showing deference to his wife's youth and educational status.

A daughter was born to the couple during their first year of marriage. Margaret Cruse died a month after the birth, leaving Thomas, a man of 50, to rear a daughter. Cruse was both indulgent and stern. When Mary was 13, her father took her to New York. The *New York Journal* described the beautiful child in headlines as the "Girl, dearest of all her father's treasures and heiress to $10,000,000." Mary was wooed by many suitors, none of whom was encouraged by Cruse. Mary died in 1913 at age 27.

After Cruse moved to Helena, Marysville continued to prosper. From 1885 to 1895, the small town reached a population of 5,000. To the hum of mine activity, the rich sounds of stamp mills and railroad train whistles were added cheers for the internationally famous baseball team, which was undoubtedly bankrolled by Cruse.

Between 1885 and the turn of the century, Marysville boasted an opera house, a railroad, six hotels, three churches, a large schoolhouse and three newspapers. Three dry goods and clothing stores, four groceries, two drug stores, two restaurants, three boot and shoe stores, three meat markets, two hardware stores, one bank, one brewery, one livery stable, two jewelry stores, one photo gallery, one furniture store, two hay and grain stores, one lumberyard, a bakery and an insurance agency lined the streets of the little town, along with 27 saloons.

Even though the town was booming, transportation was a problem. Freighting and stagecoaching were tedious and often dangerous. Wagons and stagecoaches faced a steady climb of several hours to reach the rich mines perched on steep inclines. When the Great Northern and Northern Pacific rail-

The Marysville Railroad Bridge in 1887, with the Drumlummon Mine at the left.

roads realized Marysville's potential, a race ensued to cover the 21 miles from Helena to the mining village. The Northern Pacific made the most skillful survey and secured rights to build up the most precipitous grade. An 85-foot trestle was built to span the gulch between the mines and the town. A disappointed Great Northern company was prevented from reaching the town because it could not obtain a right-of-way underneath the Northern Pacific trestle. During a blizzard on October 22, 1887, the "Helena-Northern" made its maiden run from Helena to Marysville with two cars of dignitaries aboard. After the initial run, special trains were often run to celebrate gala occasions. Thomas Cruse provided such a run for all persons in Marysville who wished to attend the laying of the capitol cornerstone on July 4, 1899.

While Cruse was the most imposing and colorful figure in Marysville's story, he was only one of many who invested in the mines that sprang up within the six mile-radius of the town.

But he alone will be remembered for his generosity to the Helena community and the state of Montana. If it had not been for Cruse's gift to St. Helena's Cathedral, it's possible that the building would not have been the magnificent structure it is today. Another act of generosity was Cruse's donation of a large amount of money for the completion of the state capitol.

Marysville today is home to a number of retirees, some of whom can trace their lineage to the town's earlier mining families. A few current residents live there because of the quiet and beauty of the environment. Some Marysville dwellers leave their homes empty in summer, but visit as weekend skiers when the snow is deep on Belmont Mountain. One of the most exciting days of the year, the annual Pioneer Picnic, is reminiscent of many celebrations of old Marysville when trainloads of merrymakers came from Helena. A full day of events today pleases everyone as in days of yesteryear.

MOUNT HELENA

BY CHERE JIUSTO

A wind-blown seed, an inch of shade, a little snow, and peace—that is all there is need for, to make a beautiful tree upon the mountain sides of Montana.
                    John Rafftery describes the blossoming
                       of Mount Helena Park, in 1905

Parks are a tradition that took root in the Old World. Under English law and the king's authority, parklands were enclosed and stocked as hunting reserves. From that root, the concept of park grew over the centuries to mean something much more democratic.

In America, the citizens of Boston created the first public park in 1630, when they set aside the Boston Common as a pasture for all. In the colonies, such green spaces served many

View from Mount Helena.

HOWARD COX PHOTOGRAPH COURTESY OF THE MONTANA HISTORICAL SOCIETY

The gazebo.

functional needs, as meeting places, parade grounds, grazing lands and gardens. And as c o m m u n i t i e s came of age, public lands set aside simply for beauty and recreation proliferated.

During the 19th century, the work of such re-nowned landscape designers as An-

Russell Aubrey Shaw and children at the Mount Helena gazebo in 1913.

drew Jackson Downing and Frederick Law Olmstead set the direction for public park design in this country. Their ideal included pastoral landscapes to be enjoyed by all. Best known for his design of New York City's Central Park in 1858, Olmstead strove to create oases of nature in urban places, where citizens could seek respite from the hubbub of everyday life.

The influences of these powerful designers spread across the nation. In Helena, farsighted vision by early town founders led to many proposals for public parks over the years, the first in 1883. Many of these never got off the drawing board, including one for a 16-mile boulevard 100 feet wide, connecting three large parks at the east, north and west edges of town. Some proposals did become reality, and that legacy remains with us today, from the wildlands of Mount Helena to the carefully manicured lawns of Hill and Women's parks to the gracious open spaces and wooded grounds of Central Park (now Green Meadow Golf Course).

It is undoubtedly Mount Helena city park that most clearly mirrors the sensibilities of those early "naturalist" landscape designers, whose work often strove to offer the best of nature, and who painstakingly designed park landscapes to appear wild and unplanned.

First proposed in 1898, by the Helena Improvement Society, Mount Helena Park was lauded as "the strangest and most interesting park project ever undertaken in this country." Taking shape on the steep slopes south of town, Mount Helena Park was birthed in the wake of heavy logging to build the young mining town, and the ashes of a major fire that burned most of the mountain in 1901. Reforestation required hand planting 30,000 conifers, trails were built to the summit and a gazebo was erected atop the peak. Other suggestions for the developing park included the planting of 300,000 flower bulbs to grow wild in the meadows, a gravity railroad and an astronomical observatory. In the end, the mountain's untamed spirit won out.

Today we love Mount Helena and continue to enjoy our mountain park much as locals were encouraged over a century ago: "If our city denizens, old and young, male and female, who complain of confinement indoors and of the dust and desolation of our streets, would indulge themselves in an hour's walk to the top of Mount Helena about the hour of sunrise or sunset they would witness a revelation of greater beauty than can be found in all the art galleries on both continents.... Do not deny yourself the health and pleasure of the moderate, but delightful walk. Go all and go often."

BRICKYARDS TO POTSHARDS

⚜

BY CHERE JIUSTO

On the west edge of Helena, along Ten Mile Creek, sprawls what was once Helena's largest brick factory. Site of the Kessler Brick and Tile Works and later the Western Clay Manufacturing Company, the brickyard since 1951 has been home to the Archie Bray Foundation, one of the most vibrant and important centers for the ceramic arts in the United States.

At the opening of the Archie Bray pottery in 1951, Charles Kessler spoke in dedication, remembering his father, Nicholas Kessler, German pioneer and brewer of fine beer. While the Kessler name today lives on with our hometown brew, Nicholas Kessler was equally important in local history as the founder of Helena's first brickworks in 1866.

Kessler Brick and Tile, first located near the old Kessler Brewery, manufactured "hand moulded" brick. These bricks were formed from mud clays dug by hand, and hauled with mule carts to a nearby horse-powered pug mill. The pug mill squeezed out the clay like a giant Playdough extruder, compressing the clay and removing the air. Then workmen pressed the milled clay into molds to form bricks. When dry, the bricks were stacked up to form their own kiln and the whole mass was fired. Soft orange and rusty-red bricks resulted and were used throughout town, many bearing the Kessler stamp.

By 1885, Kessler's clay pits played out. Seeking to continue the business, Nicholas Kessler bought out the nearby Thurston brickworks on Ten Mile Creek and their clay lode. Established by Charles C. Thurston, the Thurston works occupied the site that later became Western Clay and the Archie Bray Foundation. Charles Bray, an English brickmaker working for Thurston at

Archie Bray Foundation pottery.

the time, was placed in charge of the new Kessler brickyards, and Thurston himself went on to Anaconda where he founded a huge brickyard to supply the growing town and industry there.

During the late 1880s, Charles Bray modernized the brickyard, introducing steam power, employing brickmaking machines and boosting production. Kessler Brick and Tile fired up bricks by the millions—for such projects as the building of Fort Harrison, Marcus Daly's lower reduction works at Anaconda and the Black Eagle Smelter at Great Falls.

In the process, the brickyard grew and three great beehive kilns were added in 1897. The beehives took eight days to fire, and held vast quantities of brick and tile. Soon, however, the Thurston clays were depleted, much of which came from diggings on East Lawrence Street. A merger with the Joseph Switzer Brick and Terra Cotta Company over the Continental Divide at Blossburg was arranged in 1905. The clay at Blossburg ran deep, providing an ample supply for the business. Hauled over Mullan Pass on a Northern Pacific Railroad spur line, the clay was molded into brick and tile under the eye of Charles Bray, who became secretary and general manager of the new company, Western Clay Manufacturing. In 1920, Charles Bray bought Switzer's stock in Western Clay, and over time added five more beehive kilns. Western Clay grew to become Montana's largest manufacturer of clay products, producing bricks for building, paving and chimneys, sewer pipe, ornamental brick and tile, flower pots, lawn vases—even a clay mud facial mask—were marketed by Western Clay.

Archie Bray, son of Charles and heir to the brickyards, grew up surrounded by clay, brick and tile. Trained as a ceramic engineer in college and seasoned by a lifetime of experience in the family business, Archie Bray worked alongside his father for years and took over the operation of the brickyard with his brother Ray in 1931.

Yet Archie Bray was also a lover of art and a creative man. With the encouragement of his good friends, Peter Meloy and Branson Stevenson, Bray developed an extraordinary vision for his brickyard. Interested in handmade pots from an early age, Bray was intrigued by Pete Meloy, who dug local clay and made pots of it. Pete and his brother Hank, who was an accomplished artist, fired pots in with the bricks on numerous occasions. Archie began to dream of founding a pottery on the Western Clay Manufacturing Company grounds. With contemporary interest in native arts and handmade crafts growing, Bray's ideas meshed with a national revival of crafts and traditional arts.

Plans for the pottery took form. During the summer of 1951, two young Montana artists, Rudy Autio and Peter Voulkos, were recruited to Helena. Pete and Rudy, whose names and work are now embedded in the foundations of the American ceramic art movement, met with Archie Bray, who hired them onto the brickyard payroll.

Brickyard laborers by day, potters and sculptors by night, Autio and Voulkos dedicated themselves to helping Bray construct the pottery. With brick from the yards, and the help of many eager friends, a pottery building was erected. Into the design went richly colored, salt-glazed bricks that Archie had saved through the years, and special tiles created by several artists. A simple and compact building, the pottery contained five rooms that housed a gallery, a work studio, space for clay mixing and glazing, and the first gas-fired kiln in the state.

A foundation was created "to make available for all who are seriously and sincerely interested in any of the branches of the ceramic arts, a fine place to work," and on Archie's birthday in October 1951, the pottery was dedicated. Peter Voulkos and Rudy Autio became the first resident directors at the pottery. They were visited the following year by Bernard Leach and Shoji Hamada, world-renowned potters and venerated grandfathers of 20th-century ceramics. Their historic visit in many ways christened the pottery, and a ceramic legacy was born.

In 1953, just two years after the pottery opened, Archie Bray died. Through the years since, nine directors have kept Archie's vision, while steering the Bray through choppy waters, which included the decline of the brickyard, and ultimately, its closure.

By selling their own work, teaching classes and hosting workshops, they kept the Bray pottery open despite the failure of the brick factory. And by securing grants, loans and donations of all sizes from those who came to love and believe in the Bray, the directors placed the pottery once known as "Archie's folly" on a steady, self-sustaining course. Facilities were expanded, new resident studios and kilns were built, a thriving clay business was developed, and in 1984, the Archie Bray Foundation purchased the entire abandoned brickyard, old warehouses, beehive kilns and all.

While Archie Bray did not live to see his pottery bloom to fullness, the Archie Bray Foundation has emerged as a pinnacle of national and international ceramics. Each of the Bray's nine directors holds an established place in the world of American ceramics, and each year twenty or so resident artists from across the United States and other corners of the world are invited to the Bray. Totaling over 200 in all, the residents have come over the years to Helena, to the banks of Ten Mile Creek, to work, to share ideas and to keep the dream.

Helena's Trolleys: 1886–1928

By Dave Walter

The Helena City Commission's Transportation Coordination Committee in 1994 broached the possibility of returning trolleys to the streets of Helena. Since Helena once sported an extensive street-railway network, some historical context would benefit these discussions.

In the mid-1880s, Helena included about 10,000 residents, and it was rapidly developing an urban character. Like Butte and Bozeman, Helena's downtown district sat some distance from its Northern Pacific Railroad (N.P.) depot. A street-railway connection proved the answer in all three cities. Thus began the development of a Helena streetcar system that would last for more than 40 years.

The Helena Street Railway Company (HSRC) pioneered the field in 1886. Incorporators included Charles A. Broadwater, Charles W. Cannon, Henry M. Parchen, Anton M. Holter, Daniel A.G. Floweree, and John B. Wilson. The company's workmen laid track from Bridge Street to the N.P. depot, down the middle of Main Street and Helena Avenue. A one-way ticket cost ten cents.

Facing page, top: A Helena Electric Railway Company "single-trucker" on its way to the Broadwater Hotel and Natatorium.

Bottom: The Helena, Hot Springs and Smelter Railroad passenger car No. 2, being pulled by the Helena Motor Railway's steam dummy Capitalist *in 1889.*

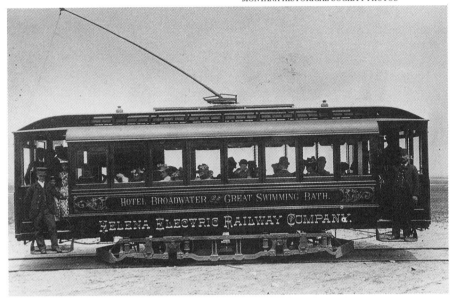

When the first horsedrawn coaches appeared on September 25, 1886, the *Helena Daily Herald* reported: "Crowds lined the streets to see the cars, and small boys hitched rides. The inauguration of the Helena Street Railway Company today marks an era in the city that foreshadows wonderful changes in all other things that presage the requirements of a great metropolis." Helenans justifiably crowed: HSRC's September 25 run marked the initiation of all street-railway transportation in Montana.

In 1889 the Helena Street Railway Company extended to five miles of track and showed a profit for the third consecutive year. The line's success drew competitors into the field. Helena realtors quickly discovered the advantages of streetcar access. As soon as tracks linked a remote addition to the business district, lot prices in the addition inflated. So, Helena real-estate men financed several city street-railway companies in the late 1880s.

Charles A. Broadwater, one of the organizers of the HSRC, incorporated the Helena Electric Railway Company (HERC) in 1890. His cars carried passengers from the downtown, from the Montana Central (Great Northern) Railway depot, and from the Northern Pacific depot to his brand-new hotel and natatorium on the west side of town.

Former Helenan Rex Myers, in his outstanding 1969 master's thesis, "The History of Street Railways in Helena, Montana, 1883-1928," notes that Broadwater's line became Montana's first operational electric street railway.

When the HERC began service on May 25, 1890, the *Helena Daily Herald* trumpeted:

"Electricity has been harnessed to do our bidding, and under its subtle force the street car glides swiftly along, enabling the owners...to scatter the blessing among the thousands."

By 1890 Helena's population had reached more than 13,000. Helenans supported four operating street railways, with two more under construction. Tracks radiated from the business district to various residential additions, as well as to the Northern Pacific depot. Three companies used horse power to pull cars, two relied on coal-burning steam "dummy" engines, and one depended on electricity. The horse-powered trains proved the most expensive to operate.

Problems, however, quickly beset these streetcar business-es. With so many companies in the field, none could turn a profit. For example, the Helena, Hot Springs and Smelter Rail-road carried almost 154,000 passengers between May 1 and November 30, 1889—and received $18,000 in gross revenue—but still fell deeper into debt.

So, during the early 1890s, Helena's sundry streetcar lines consolidated, simply to survive. The severe financial Crash of 1893 surely speeded this process. By 1894 all operations had unified as the Helena Power and Light Company (HP&L). In-corporators included Charles W. Cannon, Henry M. Parchen, Theodore H. Kleinschmidt, Charles K. Wells, Herman Gans, and Anton M. Holter—all Helenans. The new company operat-ed 20 miles of track and 24 cars, of which 16 ran on electricity and 8 rolled as trailers. HP&L retired the horses and the steam "dummy" engines.

Helena Power and Light immediately raised its city fare from a nickel to a dime, to match its charge for runs beyond the city limits. Passengers made all transfers at Sixth and Main. A trolley ride from downtown to the Broadwater Hotel took al-most 30 minutes, about the same as the trip from Sixth and Main to Montana University (North Montana Avenue and Sierra Road). A run from the business district to the N.P. depot took less than 20 minutes, at the usual rate of 6 to 9 miles per hour.

HP&L ultimately discontinued two unprofitable lines: the Lenox route located south of the Capitol (1891-1898); the run north on Villard to Forestvale Cemetery and Montana Univer-sity in the valley (1892-1899). When HP&L workmen removed the track from the valley route, however, they immediately relaid it on a new five-mile line stretching out Boulder Avenue to the smelter in East Helena.

According to its 1898 report, Helena Power and Light trol-leys traveled 185,000 miles and carried 880,952 passengers during the year. By this time the company received all of its electricity from the Missouri River dams of Samuel T. Haus-er—not incidentally a major stockholder in HP&L. In the spring of 1898, the *Herald* cooed:

"The Helena Power and Light Company is largely a home institution, most of the stocks being held here, and its officers and directors are well-known and able financiers and business-men.... There is no street railway in the Northwest giving better service."

The emergence of HP&L brought some continuity to the Helena trolley scene. Yet, although consolidation allowed HP&L to discontinue unprofitable routes and rates, it also proved detrimental, for consolidation combined the fractional debts of the many predecessor companies. Ultimately this accumulated debt—too large for local financiers to bear or to overcome—destroyed the home-owned trolley corporation.

In 1902 the Helena Light and Traction Company (HL&T) stepped up to succeed the beleaguered Helena Power and Light. This new company soon controlled not only the trolley business, but also Helena's natural gas and electric utilities. In 1905 HL&T directors avoided bankruptcy by selling the business to J.G. White and Company, headquartered in New York City. The purchaser was a Connecticut corporation with branch offices in Manila, London, and Montreal. It immediately reconstituted HL&T as the Helena Light and Railway Company (HL&R), and incorporated it in Connecticut.

Almost all Helenans failed to grasp the implications of this sale of Helena utilities to a well-heeled Eastern concern. The *Daily Independent* reduced the issue to absurdity (October 15, 1905): "The Helena Light and Railway Company puts into effect this morning its decreased street-car fare of five cents. No more red tickets, no more two-dollar books. It's a nickel if you want to ride, and that's the whole story."

But that never was "the whole story." Although the HL&R brought more than two decades of uninterrupted street-railway service to the community, it too faced major problems.

During the decade prior to World War I, the HL&R modified route alignments, maintained excellent relations with the local chapter of the Amalgamated Street Railway Employees Union, and added new electric cars to a growing fleet. In 1907 the company's rolling stock included 20 cars: 13 closed; 4 open; 2 work trailers; 1 snow plow. The 17 passenger cars traveled 373,094 miles over 18.8 miles of company track, carrying 1,820,657 customers. Helena's population at the time barely exceeded 12,000.

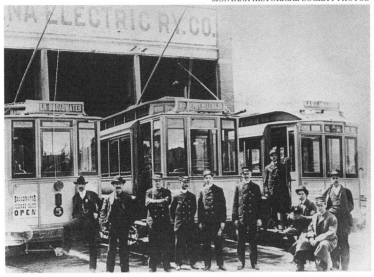

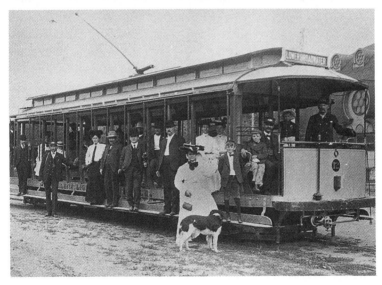

Above: The Helena Light and Traction Company's famous Big Open car (otherwise called the No. 12), posed in front of the Broadwater Natatorium in about 1908.

Top: A trio of Helena Power and Light Company's closed "single-truckers," in front of the old Helena Electric Railway car barn about 1900. Note that no two cars are exactly alike—a vestige of the patchwork history of trolley ownership in Helena during the 1890s.

Automobiles had begun operating on Helena's streets in about 1905. By 1909 they carried passengers for hire, thus competing directly with the trolleys. Although this auto competition proved profitable only during "State Fair Week" in September, it foreshadowed difficulties for Helena's streetcar system.

In 1911 the HL&R completed a new branch line to the Fairgrounds, including the construction of an underpass on Henderson Avenue beneath the Northern Pacific tracks. The company built an impressive new car barn and shop—"the finest in Montana"—in 1912 at the intersection of Main and Cutler (currently a nondescript spot between the Public Library and the Federal Building). Here it reconditioned its entire fleet to meet Progressive safety legislation passed by the state legislature.

The 1913 Montana legislature also made the Board of Railroad Commissioners the ex-officio "Public Service Commission (PSC) of Montana," with jurisdiction over public utilities. The Helena Light and Railway Company thereafter dealt with the PSC on all issues regarding increased fares, line changes and abandonments, accident investigations, and equipment modifications. Interestingly, the new commission tacitly approved the unusual monopoly that the HL&R held on the electricity, natural gas, and trolley utilities in Helena.

At least some of that approval resulted from the pride that Helenans voiced in their streetcar network. The *Helena Daily Independent* (never a paper to mince words about a reliable advertiser) noted in its "State Fair Edition" on September 21, 1913:

"The company must be reckoned among the agencies that have exerted an influence in the upbuilding of Helena and in the placing of it in the forefront of wide-awake and progressive Western municipalities. There are few, if any, towns in the West that can boast of a better-equipped street-railway system...operated by a more courteous, accommodating, and competent group of men."

Either automobile competition or inordinately rising expenses ultimately would have doomed Helena's streetcars. Because these two factors combined, the demise proved quite rapid.

In 1913 the State of Montana first licensed automobiles. Helenans registered 242 cars, and the Helena Cab Company recorded nine autos. Only four years later (1917), Helena citizens registered 1,068 vehicles; East Helenans licensed 76 more; the HL&R listed two Fords and a Hudson! The movement toward a more immediate, more flexible means of travel began to build. And the HL&R continued to run on a five-cent fare.

Throughout their existence, however, Helena's streetcar lines represented more than economics. Local groups chartered the open cars to travel the city at Christmastime, serenading neighborhoods with carols; entire clubs rode the trolleys to events at the Broadwater Plunge; Fourth of July celebrations at Central Park (northwest of the Green Meadow Country Club, along Ten Mile Creek) drew "specials" draped in flags. The sights and the sounds of the urban streetcar assured Helenans of their place in a modern, progressive America.

As operating expenses increased following World War I, the Helena Light and Railway Company annually ran at a deficit. It attempted to abandon unprofitable lines, only to meet opposition from the PSC. It proposed ticket increases, only to have those proposals slashed by the PSC. It improved its equipment, only to suffer a flurry of passenger-accident lawsuits.

As a result, HL&R customers soon realized that their electric and natural-gas payments were subsidizing the trolley system. For instance, in 1921 HL&R's overall gross revenue was $77,085, yet the street-railway deficit reached $38,658. Similarly in 1923, the entire company showed a gross income of $93,280, although the trolley line lost $33,247.

If the demise of Helena's streetcar system needed a symbolic event, it received one on December 16, 1924. At 11:20 A.M.—in a blinding blizzard, with temperatures well below zero—Great Northern steam locomotive #236 from Butte hit broadside the outbound East Helena/Smelter streetcar at the grade crossing just northeast of the Helena city limits.

The crash killed four persons on the streetcar—including the motorman, Rudolph Houle—and injured four other trolley passengers. The impact reduced car #1 to a mass of splinters, strewn along both sides of the Great Northern track for 200 yards. At the inquest, a jury ruled the tragedy accidental, resulting from "fast-falling snow, wind-whipped snow clouds, frosty windows, a haze of atmosphere, and extreme cold."

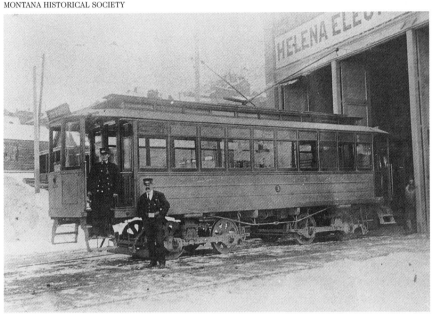

The Helena Electric Railway's famous Three Spot, *about 1910, at the old streetcar barns at Cutler and Main.*

By 1925 the collapse of the streetcar division of the Helena Light and Railway Company appeared imminent. The PSC acknowledged (Report and Order No. 1410):

"In regard to this operation, we have dealt...without success. The fortunes of the street railway ebb and ebb. Most tides turn, but this one appears to recede steadily. Motor-vehicle competition, both regulated and unregulated, is primarily responsible for the reduction in revenues. Increased fares have undoubtedly played a part, while subnormal business conditions have persuaded walking where streetcar riding was formerly a habit."

In November 1925, a U.S. District Court placed the Helena Light and Railway Company in receivership and separated its electricity and natural-gas operations from its street-railway component. The new energy company ultimately became a part of the Montana Power Company; the trolley company ultimately became a part of Helena's history. With reorganization, J.G. White and Company created the Helena Electric

Railway Company. Under its auspices, the familiar trolley cars rumbled through town for several more months.

By 1927 the streetcar line had operated at increasing deficits for nine years. Simultaneously its passenger count had dwindled markedly, from 1,500,688 in 1919 to only 736,691 in 1926. The PSC—addressing its first complete street-railway abandonment case—approved the relinquishment, effective at midnight, December 31, 1927. Motor-coach (bus) service began at 6:00 the next morning, generally adopting the trolley company's old routes.

Demolition crews salvaged most of the system's rails for resale. As required by the city, a construction company repaved the city streets and regraded the gravel roads in which tracks had been embedded. The receiver sold the three best closed cars and the last open car to the street-railway company in Great Falls. The Butte streetcar corporation purchased three other cars for its system.

During its more-than-forty years of operation (1886-1928), Helena's street-railway network evolved from numerous private lines to a consolidated local ownership to a nonresident corporation that combined multiple community utilities. This Victorian vestige of urban development and prosperity ultimately succumbed to ever-increasing operating expenses, to ever-decreasing usage, and finally to a more flexible mode of travel—the automobile.

A child of technology and financial speculation, Helena's trolley system became the victim of its own parents. Helena was the largest city in Montana in 1886 when the Helena Street Railway Company began operations; it was the smallest Montana city with trolleys when the Helena Electric Railway folded in 1927.

The 1927 abandonment threw the company's 18 employees out of work. The men held an average service record of 16 years. Steve Paterson had worked on the streetcars since 1899, when he inaugurated the East Helena run. On January 7, 1928, the company's members of the Amalgamated Association of Street and Electrical Employees, Division 495, met at the Eddy Cafe in Helena. The *Helena Daily Independent* (January 8, 1928) reported:

"The union members surrendered their charter in a melancholy gathering. They divided the cash on hand in the treasury, as well as the proceeds from the Liberty Bonds which the union bought during the World War. And they officially closed the books of an organization which has existed here for many years....

"Every man present was called upon by Joe Zoubeck, who presided as toastmaster. He swung the controller over to the last notch and signalled full speed ahead. The boys took him at his word, and they made the last trip without applying the air. If the oratorical track became a bit slippery at times, the sand box was vigorously shaken, the wheels bit into the rails, and all hands arrived safely, despite an occasional brake chain.... The members realized that it meant the breaking up of the family."

RUTTED ROAD LINKS THE GULCH AND "STATES"

※

BY JON AXLINE

Montana's 19th-century roads weren't really designed and engineered, they just kind of "growed." John Mullan's road from Fort Benton to Walla Walla, Washington was constructed between 1858 and 1862. That core travel route gave birth to a multitude of other roads in western Montana that appeared seemingly overnight as the mining camps in southwest Montana were established. Unlike the relatively smooth roads of today, many late–19th-century roads were little more than paths, infrequently maintained, rutted and filled with gaping holes. The timber bridges were little better, often exhibiting large holes in the decks and shaky foundations; it was sometimes safer (and much cheaper) to brave the torrent rather than use the bridge. To add insult to possible injury, toll keepers regularly charged outrageously high rates for using what the 1940 Montana highway map suggested were the state's "Roads to Romance."

Helena, however, was rather fortunate to be at the center of an extensive and well-developed road system. Perhaps the most important of these was the Fort Benton to Helena Road. Portions of the old route are very much in evidence today with segments still traveled by late–20th-century motorists.

The Benton Road, as it came to be known, was established shortly after gold was discovered here in 1864. The richness of the mines and economic opportunities afforded to those who chose instead to "mine the miners" quickly led to the establishment of the route as an important link between Last Chance

Gulch and the "States." By 1868, there were two Benton Roads connecting Helena with the steamboat port of Fort Benton 130 miles to the north.

Like many well-traveled roads, the Benton Road was not limited to a single track. During the summer months, the dust on the heavily used route combined with the shortage of grass for the horses, mules and oxen would have caused the users to fan out. The Benton Road, therefore, probably cut a wide swath across the Prickly Pear and Little Prickly Pear valleys. According to legend, Ten Mile Creek got its name because it was ten miles from Silver City, the valley's first population center before the discovery of Last Chance Gulch. The creek provided a mile marker of sorts to the freighters and coachmen who used the road.

MONTANA HISTORICAL SOCIETY

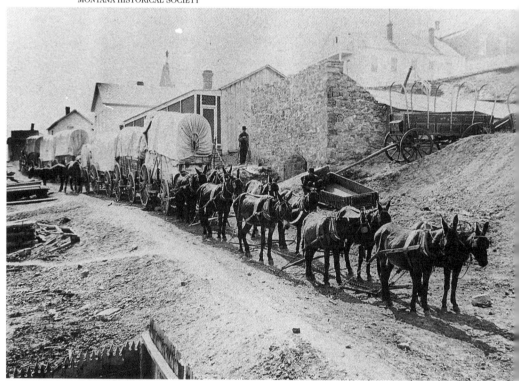

Vawter Street after 1874.

Both incarnations of the Benton Road utilized a portion of the older Mullan Road. The first Benton Road followed the Mullan Road down the Little Prickly Pear Creek, passed by where the Chevallier Ranch is now located and continued down the existing county road to the vicinity of the present Silver City bar. From there, the route followed Birdseye Road down to the junction

Diamond R freight train (Kirkendall Train) in Prickly Pear Canyon.

of the Mullan Pass road. They then split, with the Benton Road continuing to Helena along Birdseye Road and then Country Club Avenue. Because the Civil War diverted the government's attention elsewhere, the Mullan Road fell into disrepair soon after it was completed in 1862. After gold was discovered in Montana, however, the lure of easy profits caused toll companies to adopt and sometimes improve sections of the road. The Prickly Pear Wagon Road Company was the first to assume control of the Mullan Road from the vicinity of the Wolf Creek Canyon to Helena.

King and Gillette purchased the toll-road license from the company in 1866. They then constructed an alternate route to Last Chance Gulch for about $50,000 and were able to re-

coup their expenditure within two years. The new road generally followed the present Lincoln Road into the Helena Valley.
It then meandered across the valley east of North Montana
Avenue before crossing the thoroughfare at the southern bound-
ary of Resurrection Cemetery. After angling through the old
dredge tailings, it struck off for Last Chance Gulch via McHugh
Lane, Villard and North Main Street. This road was a primary
arterial into the city until the completion of the Northern Pacific Railroad in 1883. Because the new road lacked the steep
grades of its predecessor, it was much easier to negotiate and
therefore more popular with the freighters.

Once the wagons reached Helena, they were forced to camp
outside of town, near the present location of the railrod depot;
the narrowness of the gulch prevented its heavy use. A feeling
for this can still be experienced by anyone who tries to navigate Last Chance Gulch during the morning delivery times for
the local bars and restaurants.

Helena folklore reports that Benton Avenue (called Senior
Street before 1887) is the old Fort Benton to Helena Road.
While portions of it may have been, the rock retaining walls
adjacent to South Park were associated with the Unionville to
Park City Road from Helena. The retaining walls do not appear in an 1875 street map of the city, but are apparent in an
1885 photograph of the Reeder's Alley area. It is not presently
known who constructed them, but the road that tops the old
walls was definitely designed for wagon traffic and not for today's automobiles. A component of that road, the Morelli Bridge,
at the head of Reeder's Alley, was constructed about 1880, sug-
gesting that the retaining walls were built about the same time.
The Morelli Bridge is the oldest bridge still in use in Montana.

Travelers on the roads of today miss much of the adventure sojourners of the late 1800s experienced on Montana's
primitive roads and bridges. Luckily, we can still experience
the old Benton Road and keep our fillings intact.

BUILDINGS

"The Guardian of the Gulch" A Story of Use and Preservation

BY DAVE WALTER

Helena's Fire Tower—"The Guardian of the Gulch"—remains one of the community's exemplary preservation successes. This unusual structure anchors the downtown district and has become a distinctive symbol for the City of Helena.

The story of the Fire Tower is replete with the community's frontier spirit and its sense of the past.

The several devastating fires that swept Last Chance Gulch in the late 1860s and early 1870s might have finished another mining camp. Helenans, however, switched quickly from placer mining to banking, merchandising, and freighting—and they

Helena's Watch Tower.

MONTANA HISTORICAL SOCIETY

determined to make their fledgling community permanent and prosperous.

Immediately following the camp's first blazes, mining-district leaders hung a large triangle on a rack at the corner of Bridge and Water streets and struck it to call volunteers to the bucket brigade. By 1868 they had moved the triangle rack to Tower Hill.

Following a series of severe fires in 1869, civic fathers hired a watchman to sit on Tower Hill each night. He benefited from an absolutely remarkable panorama—one Helenans still enjoy today. The next year they built a flimsy lookout stand atop the knoll for the watchman. Thus Helena's observation platform became the community's first piece of municipal property. Concerned townsmen installed the first bell on a new rack adjacent to the lookout in 1873, greatly expanding the alarm area.

The original version of the current "Guardian" cost $100 to construct in 1874. Its necessity had been underscored by the devastating blaze of January 9. The *Helena Daily Herald* observed (March 19, 1874):

"The plan, as drawn by Holter and Bro., will give us a tower 15 feet higher than the old one, and in every respect superior and more substantial. It is to be built in a manner that will defy the strongest wind, which of itself is no small consideration, as the old tower was and still is liable to blow down at almost any time.... The building is to be immediately constructed and when completed will be an ornament to the city as well as indispensable to our safety."

The city installed a much larger, heavier bell—the grand silver bell currently sitting in the south approach to the Civic Center—in a reinforced Fire Tower in 1886. At this time two of the community's most trusted men held the job of lookout, at the rate of $75 per month.

Each watchman sat a 12-hour shift in a swivel chair in the Tower's cupola, slowly scanning the town for smoke in the wrong place. He kept a small heater stove for warmth in winter, and he opened all the windows for summer ventilation. When sounding an alarm, he could code the ward where the fire was burning and then provide a continuous warning to clear the streets for the horsedrawn fire engines.

A view of Helena from Tower Hill.

Helena brought its watchmen down from the Fire Tower in the early 1890s, when it developed a signal system that combined electrical alarm boxes and telephones to deliver the alarm to the firehouse. Nevertheless, for decades, a fireman climbed the lookout's steep, rickety stairs each evening to ring the 8:45 curfew, dreaded by generations of Helena's youngsters.

In 1931 the alarm bell's mechanism froze, putting an end to the sonorous curfew. Yet more serious consequences derived from the earthquakes of October 1935. The Fire Tower had suffered substantial structural damage, leading some townsmen to advocate its demolition. In response, a group of Helena women created the Helena Landmarks Association and focused public attention on the restoration and preservation of the Tower.

This group, led by Marguerite Greenfield, successfully raised money for repairs. It ultimately saved the Tower as a historical symbol—a dominating reminder of the placer-gold origins of the Capital City.

In 1950 a lightning fire weakened the deteriorating structure and, for safety, the Fire Department removed the Tower's two bells. A committee of the Helena Chamber of Commerce, under the leadership of L.P. Barney, then rehabilitated the Tower, with time and materials donated by Helena businesses.

The Last Chance Gulch Restoration Association succeeded the Chamber. By raising public funds during the early 1960s, LCGRA members Jean Galusha and Betty Doering organized a series of repairs to the Tower. The group's efforts were recognized in 1964—during Helena's centennial—when "the Guardian of the Gulch" became the City's official symbol. It remains Helena's emblem—just take a look at the City letterhead or the passenger doors of City vehicles.

During the early 1970s, members of Soroptimist International of Helena embraced the Fire Tower as a long-term project. Their fund-raising and public-education activities were rewarded in 1972, when the Tower received listing on the National Register of Historic Places.

The Helena Fire Department in 1908.

Gradually the Soroptimists improved the Tower Hill site, erecting the current fencing in the 1970s and providing illumination of the Tower in 1987. The organization's most ambitious campaign in behalf of "the Guardian" began in 1990, when the City Engineer estimated that $25,000 would be needed to restore the Fire Tower to acceptable standards.

First the City of Helena's Parks Department applied for and received a $5,000 grant from the Montana Historical Society's State Historic Preservation Office. Then a Soroptimist committee, under the leadership of Delores Hill, embarked on a series of fund-raising efforts that included raffles, T-shirt and belt-buckle sales, and fire-house pancake breakfasts. With the donations of Helena's students, private citizens, businesses, service groups, and clubs, they reached their incredible goal of $20,000.

The Soroptimists supervised major restoration work on the

Fire Tower itself in 1991, as well as some important landscaping of Tower Hill. The restoration is first-rate work, and all Helena owes the Soroptimists an enormous debt of gratitude. In 1994 the group commenced a $5,000 fund-raising effort to replace the fencing around "the Guardian" and to add interpretive signage to Tower Hill.

From many points in downtown Helena, one can look up today and see "the Guardian of the Gulch"—as one has been able to see it for the last 120 years. This structure remains a distinctive reminder of Helena's frontier era, and it still anchors the downtown district.

Fortunately this landmark survives—but only because of the courage and diligence of a series of Helena individuals and groups through the years. We all continue to benefit from their foresight and commitment.

⁘

Contributions to the continuing effort to protect and preserve "the Guardian of the Gulch" for future generations can be sent to: Soroptimist International Fire Tower Fund, P.O. Box 1216, Helena (59624).

⁘

In researching this piece, the author relied heavily on the expertise and assistance of Soroptimist committee chair Delores Hill, local-history expert Eula May Hall, and Parks Department Superintendent Rich Lynd. Thank you all very much for your knowledge, kindness, and cooperation.

CENTRAL SCHOOL: OLD No. 1

BY ELLEN BAUMLER

Children will spill out the doors of Central School at 402 N. Warren Street today just as they have every school day for more than a century. The approaching end of another school year is a good time to reflect on the role these grounds played in Helena's early history and recount some memories generated here.

Helena High's first graduating class—Ida Wilson, Anna Warfield, and Mary Wheeler.

MONTANA HISTORICAL SOCIETY

Professor Wheeler wrote from Pennsylvania that he would "like to visit dear old Helena again. It would seem like home to me. I keep a picture of old No. 1 Schoolhouse hanging up in my house yet."

In January of 1876 the momentous dedication of Helena's newest schoolhouse gave the capital city the lead in establishing quality public instruction. Helena Graded School Number One was the first in the territory to separate students by grade and to offer a high school curriculum. The opening of the $25,000 building made the educational facilities of Montana Territory "...equal to those of many of the old communities in the States." The Legislative Assembly, Supreme Court justices, other dignitaries and hundreds of well-wishers turned out as school board trustee Wilbur F. Sanders transferred the keys to the first principal, Professor C.L. Wheeler.

Long-time Helena physician Rudolph Horsky, one of the school's first primary-grade students, shared some of his recollections in an 1890s address. He recalled that Graded Number One was the "largest, finest...most pretentious structure in the town," and that it was not Professor Wheeler's erudition that impressed the students, but rather his "long whiskers." He remembered how every morning the students, arranged by grade from primary to high school, marched to the assembly room. The younger boys were enamored of the piano accompanist who, according to her female contemporaries, was "too large for her dress." This young lady had a habit of fainting as the last high school boy filed past, thus requiring his assistance. With schoolboy wisdom, the boys concluded that she must have had "designs" on him. And in retrospect, Horsky admits to "the plausibility of the older girls' reasoning" that her clothing was too tight.

Anna Warfield, Mary C. Wheeler and Ida Wilson were the first students to complete the prescribed three-year high school course. Granville Stuart, Cornelius Hedges and Colonel Sanders were among the speakers at their impressive graduation ceremonies in 1879. Misses Warfield and Wheeler returned to teach at Graded Number One the following year. Miss Wheeler, a celebrated artist, went on to devote forty years to the Helena Public Schools supervising art education.

When Montana achieved statehood in 1889, city fathers reasoned that a visibly flourishing community would increase Helena's chances in the bid for state capital. Voters agreed, approving a million-dollar bond issue to build a new high school in 1890. By 1892, the new Helena High School, a public library and a public auditorium that rivaled even those of sophisticated Eastern cities sprawled across the block on either side of Central School (as it was now called).

Helena indeed became the capital in 1894, and enormous crowds choked the Warren Street Auditorium during the victory celebrations. Soon after, Professor Wheeler wrote from Pennsylvania to a former student that he would "like to visit dear old Helena again. It would seem like home to me. I keep a picture of old No. 1 Schoolhouse hanging up in my house yet." The professor would certainly not have recognized the crowded block.

One April night in 1893 a strange thing happened. The 1860s mining camp cemetery had originally occupied this block, and so construction of the graded school in 1875 had entailed moving the graves to the new cemetery on Benton Avenue. One, however, was missed. A sizable landslide on the south side of Lawrence Street exposed the coffin of an early-day resident dressed in rough miner's clothing. The tall fellow was unusually well-preserved, and his red hair and whiskers had grown quite long. One can only imagine the stories that circulated among the students. The newspapers, however, barely mentioned the story, and he was quickly reburied in the Benton Avenue Cemetery.

The 1890s buildings are long gone and the present Central School, built between 1915 and 1921, has replaced its predecessor. Now it's backpacks instead of bookstraps, but Central's students haven't changed much. Most would agree that it's a great place to build a second century of memories.

QUARRIED STONE FOR A SENSE OF WEALTH AND STABILITY

BY JON AXLINE

The Thomas Kain and Sons Company, and its successor, the Kain Granite Company, was one of only a few stone quarries in the area that supplied construction material to Helena's builders during the community's early history. The demand for stone created a boom in the quarrying business as Helenans strove to make their community more permanent and visually attractive in the wake of several disastrous conflagrations in the 1860s and 1870s. The stone buildings provided a feeling of wealth and stability to the young metropolis. The city, moreover, was ideally located near some of the finest sources of the material in the state.

Some of the city's earliest quarries bordered the Gulch. Many, like the Adami Brothers on Clore (now Park) Street, literally quarried the material in their backyards for use as building foundations and relatively simple structures (the Adamis may also have provided the stone for the retaining walls lining the west side of South Park). By the late 1880s and early 1890s, however, the building boom that preceded the economic depression of 1893 created a demand for better-quality building stone. The Kain family was quick to take advantage of the opportunity and soon left a permanent record of their endeavors on the community.

Born in Scotland in 1842, Thomas McKain trained as a master stonemason in Liverpool. In 1885, he and his two older sons scouted the Helena area for sources of granite and obtained land adjacent to Ten Mile Creek near Baxendale. By about 1890, the entire family had arrived in the Helena area and the "Mc" was dropped from the last name. Until 1903 when the Kains built a substantial stone house near Baxendale, the family lived in primitive accommodations near the quarries. The company was family-owned and operated, with Thomas serving as president, while his sons, Henry and John, were vice-president and manager respectively.

By 1908, Thomas Kain & Sons was firmly established in Helena and was aggressively marketing their product throughout Montana from their headquarters at 345 North Main. Partially through the Kains' efforts, Lewis and Clark County was the largest producer of granite in the state before World War I. Shortly after the turn of the century, however, it became obvious to Kain that the Ten Mile quarries were nearly depleted of substantial building stone. The company found an alternate source near Clancy at Shingle Gulch, and after about 1905, the majority of the building stone quarried by the Kains came from that quarry. The Ten Mile quarries, apparently, were mainly used to supply stone for funerary purposes. During their years of greatest activity, the Kain company employed 75 men housed in dormitories near both quarries.

The firm thrived in the 1900s. In late 1909, the state announced plans to add two wings to the Capitol and solicited bids for the building stone. The Kain company submitted three bids in January 1910—one from each quarry owned by the firm—and was awarded the contract the following month. According to the agreement, the Kains promised "…delivery of granite in sufficient quantity to reach the gables or roof by October 1 and the entire supply called for in the bids by November 1…" The stone came from the Shingle Gulch quarry at a cost of $192,890 (including delivery). Whether the company met their deadlines is not known as the stonecutters and other "granite workmen" went on strike that summer.

The Capitol contract enabled the Kains to expand their business. Thomas Kain and Sons was renamed Kain Granite Company in 1911 and a new showroom and office building was constructed the following year. The company's building still stands at

Kain Granite works west of Helena.

Kain's Granite Quarry.

the corner of Seventh Avenue and Jackson Street and is now occupied by the Acupuncture & Acupressure Health Clinic.

A 1912 article in the *Helena Independent* described the Kain Granite Company shop near the railroad tracks on Benton Avenue as "one of the most up-to-date establishments of its kind in the country, having all the latest devices for handling and cutting granite, marble and other stone." Its location next to the Northern Pacific and Great Northern railroad tracks gave the company an advantage over other stonecutting firms in Helena.

The shop machinery was contained in two large sheds, one housing the surfacing machine and the other a 5-ton overhead crane and pneumatic cutting tools. The cutters, surfacing machine and polishers were powered by a 75 horsepower electric motor. From six to ten men were employed at the plant with a combined daily payroll of $150—pretty good wages for the time.

During its peak between the mid-1890s and late 1920s, the Kain Granite Company provided cut and finished stone locally and to ventures throughout Montana. Although the list is far from complete (the company's records have not yet surfaced), some of the buildings and structures in Helena include the City-County Building (1898), Placer Hotel (1913), Kain Building (1912) and the receiving vault, arch and Brown Mausoleum at Forestvale Cemetery (1890–circa 1895). The company is responsible for about 10 percent of the granite monuments at Forestvale, including John X. Beidler's massive rough-cut headstone. Ironically, when Thomas Kain died in 1917, he was buried across the road from Forestvale at the Odd Fellows Cemetery—an organization in which he was an active member for much of his life.

The Kains' contributions to Montana's "built environment" were not confined to Helena. The company also provided stone to Governor Robert Smith's monument in Kalispell, the Brooks Mausoleum in Lewistown, St. Marks Episcopal Church in Havre, the Boulder River School and Hospital and the county courthouses in Forsyth and Philipsburg.

By the 1930s, however, the economic depression and increasing use of reinforced concrete instead of building stone contributed to a decline in the Kain Granite Company's fortunes. Beginning in 1931, it becomes increasingly obvious in the city directories that the company concentrated on the manufacture of graveyard monuments. By 1939 it was the only monument company and quarry listed in the city directory. The company made its last appearance in the 1956 Helena city directory.

Thomas Kain and the Kain Granite Company significantly contributed to the Helena we see today. In the days before reinforced and prestressed concrete, stone was the building material of choice for many of Helena's property owners. While the extent of the company's impact to the city's built environment is not known, what remains provides a good illustration of its legacy to our historical character. That the quarries were vitally important can also be seen in the number of stone foundations, commercial buildings and homes that grace the Queen City of the Rockies.

ST. HELENA SCHOOL AROSE WITH CATHEDRAL

BY LEANNE KURTZ

Dwarfed by the ornate St. Helena Cathedral and currently home to several pigeons who have assembled nests at the top of the pillars framing the doorway, the St. Helena School stands as evidence of the history and development of Catholic education in the area.

MONTANA HISTORICAL SOCIETY

St. Helena School, dedicated in 1909.

Bishop John Patrick Carroll was selected by Rome as the successor to Bishop Brondel, who had served Helena's congregation for 19 years. Installed at the Helena Cathedral of the Sacred Heart in 1905, one of Bishop Carroll's first priorities was the expansion of Catholic institutions. Accomplishments during his reign included new quarters for the House of the Good Shepherd, improvements at St. John's Hospital, St. Vincent's Academy for young women and the opening in 1906 of St. Aloysius Institute for boarders, the boys' equivalent to St. Vincent's. In addition to these undertakings, Bishop Carroll is also largely credited with the notable expansion of Catholic education in early twentieth-century Helena.

In 1907, seeking to actively expand the church's role in the education of Helena's youth, Bishop Carroll proposed the construction of the cathedral on land donated by Colonel Thomas Cruse and, concurrently, a primary school on the adjacent block. Relying on an initial $25,000 from Cruse and a considerably successful fund drive, the cathedral and school alike were completed at a total cost of $752,000. A.O. Von Herbulis served as architect for both the cathedral and the school. Bishop Carroll assumed the role of contractor, personally overseeing construction after dismissing the firm originally hired for the job.

Monsignor Victor Day, appointed by Bishop Carroll as chairman of the committee to oversee fund-raising for the two structures, officially dedicated St. Helena School on September 7, 1909, and classes commenced the next day. The Sisters of Charity of Leavenworth staffed the new school in addition to their other duties at St. Aloysius, St. Ann's Infants Home, and St. Vincent's Academy. The innovative new school building provided its first classes and many students afterwards with athletic facilities and a stage as well as large classrooms and club meeting rooms. Bishop Carroll hoped to augment the students' basic education by encouraging wholesome recreational opportunities.

St. Helena School served as a grade school from 1909 to 1936. When the 1935 earthquake damaged St. Vincent's Academy, the high-school girls in attendance there were moved to the St. Helena building. The girls finished the year occupying club rooms previously used by the Knights of Columbus. In 1936, Bishop Gilmore announced establishment of Cathedral High School, a coeducational high school combining the girls from St. Vincent's Academy with the boys attending Carroll High School. Father James G. Tougas administered the remodeling and redecorating of the St. Helena school building, adding laboratory equipment, more classroom space and an auditorium. In the fall of 1936, 125 students began their school year at Cathedral High School. For 18 years, the original buff-colored brick building now on the corner of Warren and Eleventh housed Catholic students of all grade levels.

By 1954, the high school had outgrown its quarters, warranting the construction of the addition that fronts Warren Street and runs along Eleventh Avenue. From 1954 to 1969, Cathedral High School students excelled at journalism, public speaking, music, theater and sports, earning numerous academic as well as athletic honors. Citing financial difficulties as the reason, Bishop Hunthausen announced that both schools would close at the end of the 1969 academic year. Since then space has been leased to various agencies and organizations (including a little room in the basement where yours truly attended kindergarten).

The St. Helena school building faces an uncertain future, but will likely endure in the memories of the students who sang in the choir, played basketball, wrote for the school paper and studied chemistry under its roof. In the shadow of St. Helena Cathedral, the school building continues to serve as testimony to Bishop Carroll's commitment to the minds, bodies and spirits of Helena's Catholic youth.

TEMPLE EMANU-EL: FIRST TEMPLE AMIDST THE ROCKIES

BY ELLEN BAUMLER

The former Temple Emanu-El at 515 North Ewing Street was the pride and joy of Helena's Jewish community, symbolizing the end of a long struggle to acquire a permanent place of worship. But the stately building was also meant as a gift to the entire community, "to ornament the city we love." Dedicated in 1891, it was the first Jewish synagogue built between St. Paul and Portland.

Jewish pioneers like Morris Silverman, Henry Klein, Moses Morris and Samuel Schwab came from Prussia, Austria and Bavaria looking for a place to call home. Opportunity drew these and many other immigrants to the West while business as well as religious beliefs brought Jewish settlers together. In the 1860s Helena's Jewish residents founded the Hebrew Benevolent Association, a "working charity," which long fostered an active commitment to the greater Helena community.

Determination was a frontier necessity well demonstrated by Jewish businessmen like Polish-born Marcus Lissner, who ran Helena's highly acclaimed International Hotel. Lissner's remarkable spirit and energy were a marvel; his uninsured hotel burned and was rebuilt so many times during the 1860s and 1870s that it became known as "the Phoenix."

Nor was fire unconquerable to Jacob Feldberg. When his

TEMPLE OF CONGREGATION EMANU-EL, HELENA, MONTANA

People of all creeds filled the temple for its dedication in 1891.

clothing business burned in 1869, he promptly rebuilt. And when the fire of 1871 threatened his residence, Feldberg became a hero. Firefighters told the small-statured merchant that he was not "big enough to fight fires." Yelling at everyone he could find, Feldberg gathered forces, jumped from a roof into a neighbor's burning kitchen, and grabbed all the pans and pails in sight. The resulting bucket brigade saved the neighborhood, and Feldberg was later dubbed "Helena's Paul Revere."

Twenty percent of the Board of Trade membership in 1877 was Jewish. Jews served in public offices (Marcus Lissner was elected to the city council six times), and they were respected by the gentile community. Professions included lawyers, bankers, merchants and service providers. Unlike other independent businessmen, Jewish merchants in particular helped stabilize a vulnerable economy because they worked together, and, as part of a far-reaching financial network, had access to capital beyond the immediate community.

By the end of the 1880s, the congregation held strong as a second generation came of age and immigrants continued to bolster the population. In 1890, the dream of building a "temple amidst the Rockies" reached fruition when Governor J.K. Toole laid the cornerstone. Architects Heinlein and Mathias designed the Romanesque-style synagogue, which is constructed of porphyry, sandstone and granite. Its sanctuary had a 30-foot ceiling and seating capacity of 300 with removable galleries increasing capacity to 500.

People of all creeds filled the Temple Emanu-El at its dedication. Also in attendance were most of the "little band of followers...who kept alive the religion of their forefathers" for more than twenty-four years. Josephine Israel (who later married Sol Hepner and, among other important community contributions, helped found Shodair Hospital) handed the keys to congregation president Herman Gans. In a moving address, Gans explained that "the Jewish heart is ever loyal to the god of the fathers...no matter how far removed from a religious center," but his joy and gratitude for overcoming seemingly insurmountable difficulties were evident.

Within the decade, however, economic difficulties and lack of local job opportunities diminished the congregation. By the 1930s it could no longer maintain the magnificent synagogue. Norman Winestine, leader of the small group, sadly arranged the sale of the temple to the State of Montana: the price was a token one dollar and a promise to keep the building in use.

The state readied the temple for its new function as offices for Social and Rehabilitation Services by stripping it of all religious symbolism. Removal of the Hebrew inscription meaning "Gate to the Eternal" cut in stone over the entrance and the beautiful star-studded "onion" domes visually divested Helena of a significant part of its cultural heritage.

The temple building stood vacant from 1976 to 1980. Fearing its eventual demolition, Norman Winestine was "terribly discouraged and disappointed" when the state put it up for sale. But when the Catholic Diocese of Helena purchased the building for $83,000, the state more than recouped its small investment, and everyone came out ahead. Indeed, I think that

Norman Winestine would be pleased to see the beloved Temple Emanu-El in useful service and so well maintained.

Besides the synagogue, Helena possesses one other reminder of this once-vibrant community. North of town tucked away from traffic is the Home of Peace Cemetery where most of Helena's Jewish pioneers rest. The modern visitor cannot help but be impressed with the names on the headstones: Lissner, Schwab, Morris, Silverman, Klein, Feldberg, Gans, Israel, Hepner, Winestine and many others. Arranged by family with one group close to its neighbor, the orderly rows represent the once-living congregation that contributed so much to our community.

FAREWELL
TO THE
MARLOW

❧⚜❧

BY HARRIETT C.
MELOY

One of the sorriest days in Helena's rich cultural history was
May 9, 1972, when a wrecking crew began its assault on the city's
favorite entertainment center, the Marlow Theater.

Weeks before the building's demise, the theater marquee was
blank, the interior halls and ramps silent. When workmen were
asked the reason for the building's destruction, they said they believed the structure was being ripped down to enlarge a street for
urban renewal.

An onlooker, who happened to be an apprentice carpenter
when the theater was constructed, described the building's foundation: On three sides, four-foot concrete piers were sunk 54 feet
into the ground. Eight of these piers spanned each side of the
building and four stretched across the back. The Marlow had
been built to last; demolition could take a month or six weeks, according to the onlooker's prediction.

Six weeks? Only a breath of time to destroy what had begun
as one man's vision almost a century earlier.

Thomas A. Marlow, president of the National Bank of Montana and well-known Helena entrepreneur, was the dreamer who
wrote to another visionary, John S.M. Neill, in 1908, describing
plans to build a theater in Helena, a playhouse to be complete and
modern in every detail. Neill, publisher of the *Helena Independent,* promised any assistance his newspaper could give.

Neill's efforts, supported by enthusiasm as well as money
from many other Montanans, helped Marlow raise more than

Helenans enjoyed stage plays, movies, theatrical events, fashion shows, and even political candidates parading across the Marlow's impressive theater stage.

$85,000 during the next few years. Cost of the building was to be $100,000, but the final figure exceeded that by at least half again.

An architect, H. Ryan, designer of handsome theaters in Seattle and Butte, took charge of the construction. Most of the building supplies were purchased in Helena. Perhaps the new building even met present-day requirements to provide access for the disabled, since ramps were installed from the main floor to the mezzanine and on up to the balcony. As reported in the *Helena Independent* the ladies room on the mezzanine, spacious and heavily carpeted, was furnished with comfortable lounges and chairs.

The orchestra pit was unusually large to accommodate numerous musicians for vaudeville performances and musical plays. A Wurlitzer organ was placed beneath the screen to give background sound for silent movies.

Before the Marlow opened, legitimate theater had been missing from Helena's cultural diet for a number of years, perhaps as far back as when the Ming Theater on Jackson Street presented Katie Putnam and John Maguire, two highly popular stage stars. Theater-goers accustomed to movie prices were not prepared to pay $10 for an opening night ticket at the new Marlow. People thought there must be some mistake about the opening show ticket price. But pay the price they did, for on April 3, 1918, the night of the grand opening, every ticket was sold for the musical comedy "A Show of Wonders" from the New York Winter Garden. Theater manager Connie Eckhart claimed the performance would be as "magnificent a spectacle" as a Helena audience had ever seen. To conform with the war theme on everyone's mind, a final scene, "Over the Top," depicted a raid on German trenches by American aeroplanes—and "a marvelous air battle between the Americans and the Huns."

Thomas Marlow, who occupied one of the boxes with other Helena showgoers, remained modestly in the background as E.C. Day made a dedicatory speech to celebrate the new building. When Marlow did rise to greet the audience, he asked permission to "write off the deficit of $40,000," which still remained to be paid.

Over the next half-century, rich entertainment was served to the people of Helena. Stage plays, movies, Helena theatrical events, fashion shows from leading Helena merchants, and even political candidates paraded across the impressive theater stage.

With a wistful sense of *déjà vu,* Helenans recall the late 1930s when Eva LeGallienne, recognized as a force in American theater, brought members of the American Repertory Theatre to Helena and played the lead part in *Hedda Gabler.* During the 1940s Alfred Lunt and Lynne Fontanne, reputed to be the best acting couple on the American stage, appeared at the Marlow. In the summer of 1960, presidential hopeful John F. Kennedy asked for support of Montanans during the Democratic State Convention held in the Marlow.

Gary Cooper and Myrna Loy greeted fellow Helenans from the Marlow's stage during visits to their hometown.

In its heyday the theater brought to Helena the finest plays and movies of the era, but the final movie shown at the Marlow on March 26, 1972, was *Toklat,* a story of a bear, described as wholesome family entertainment. (Does anyone remember *Toklat*?)

In spirit, Helena's half-century love affair with the Marlow will never end. Nor will Helenans entirely forgive an organization referred to as "Urban Renewal" for destroying one of our most enriching and important cultural resources. No other building or institution will ever take its place.

EVENTS

HELENA'S GREATEST CELEBRATION EVER!

DAVE WALTER

Many Helena residents live in the area today because of a remarkable event that occurred a century ago, on November 6, 1894. On that Election Tuesday, Helena defeated Anaconda to become the permanent capital of the fledgling state of Montana.

After a vicious campaign that pitted "Copper Kings" Marcus Daly and William A. Clark against each other, Helena received 51.83 percent of the 52,142 votes cast. It won by a narrow plurality of 1,906 votes: 27,024 to 25,118.

Daly reportedly spent $2.5 million backing Anaconda. Clark and Helena's leaders—particularly Samuel T. Hauser, Wilbur Fisk Sanders, Martin Maginnis, Thomas H. Carter, Anton M. Holter, and the Toole brothers—countered with a $500,000 war chest, a statewide "Speakers Bureau," and a powerful "Women's Helena-for-Capital Committee." Rampant corruption marked the campaign, and each vote cost its respective supporters about $55.

The tension built in the streets of Helena throughout Election Day. Early on Tuesday evening, returns began dribbling into "Helena for Capital" campaign offices, private homes, and the Auditorium on special telegraph lines. At the *Helena Independent* building on lower Broadway, a reporter immediately transferred the figures to stereopticon slides and projected them out a third-floor window (*Daily Independent,* November 7, 1894):

"All Helena seemed downtown. People ate their dinners at an unusually early hour and hurried to the business portion of the city to get the latest capital returns. The local and state elections were nearly forgotten, for all interest centered in the capital vote.

"The greatest enthusiasm prevailed. The people were excited and they did not care who knew it. Dignified old gentlemen shouted and swung their hats like 12-year-old lads when some particularly encouraging election news was shown out on the great canvas stretched on the Masonic Building, opposite the Independent Building. The street was black with people and loud shouts for Helena were heard on every hand."

An estimated 1,500 people packed Broadway and Main streets during the evening. They celebrated continuously as early returns built a comfortable lead for Helena. By 11:00 P.M., however, reports began arriving from Anaconda strongholds, and the margin disappeared. The contest remained "too close to call" at 3:00 A.M., when a persistent drizzle finally dispersed the crowd.

On Wednesday morning, as darkness turned to cold, rainy half-light, hundreds of apprehensive Helenans regrouped on lower Broadway. All the onlookers awaited the final returns from Butte, for that city held the key. Helena supporters had conceded Butte's majority to Daly—but, if Helena could reduce Anaconda's margin of victory there, it might capture the election.

Shortly after noon on Wednesday, the Butte figures clattered in. Helena had snatched a surprising 40 percent of the Butte vote! All of the work, strategy, and money that Clark and John M. Quinn, the editor of Clark's *Butte Miner,* had poured into Helena's campaign had defeated Daly in his own bailiwick. The amazing Butte tally—when combined with late-arriving rural votes from eastern Montana—assured Helena the permanent capital, despite a terribly slender margin.

A spontaneous celebration on Wednesday night involved about 2,500 Helena residents. The crowds coursed around the downtown district from early evening until 4:00 A.M. Much of the revelry occurred in the saloons, but local bands marched

By Monday, November 12, Helena had received "the greatest influx of visitors in its history" for the parade and official celebration.

this way and that through the night, while fireworks exploded erratically overhead.

During the evening, downtown intersections offered the triumphant soapbox speeches of: Helena "Speakers Bureau" heroes Joseph K. and Warren Toole, Thomas Carter, Sam Word, and young Tom Walsh; noted Marysville orator Joe Oker; George Woodson, the leader of the "Colored Citizens for Helena" group. The crowd's mood remained absolutely euphoric through the night. The *Helena Herald* remarked that the festivities were "the first in which we have seen women marching!"

On Thursday, November 8, civic leaders set Helena's official celebration for the following Monday, November 12. This schedule not only provided local organizers the time to prepare, but it also gave Helena's supporters from around the

Annie Lehner, aged six, was a princess in waiting to the Queen of Helena at the 1894 victory celebration.

state the time to travel to the Capital City. The Northern Pacific Railroad Company immediately offered a half-price round-trip fare for any Montanan who wanted to attend the celebration. James J. Hill and the Great Northern Railway (who had supported Daly and Anaconda) reluctantly matched the offer.

Helena's preparations proved very elaborate. The "Helena for Capital" Committee booked speakers for the various gatherings; the Women's Capital Club decorated the Auditorium and the Opera House and prepared for the receptions at each; the Young Men's Capital Club organized the parade, arranged accommodations for out-of-town visitors, and gathered hundreds of torches. A small committee collected every bit of fireworks in Helena, Butte, Great Falls, and Missoula—including 500 pounds of "red fire."

Another group of Helenans laid a bonfire atop Mount Helena, using 10 cords of wood and 50 gallons of coal oil. They prepared two smaller piers on the flanks of the mountain...just in case. Businesses decorated their storefronts, many residences draped bunting from their windows and porches, and workers hung Chinese lanterns both downtown and along the parade route. On Saturday celebrants erected three huge arches over Main Street, between Sixth and Broadway, honoring Clark, Hauser, Quinn, and the "Friends of Helena."

By Monday, November 12, Helena had received "the greatest influx of visitors in its history"—either before or since. In 1894 the city's population exceeded 12,000; but by Monday an additional 5,500 revelers had descended on Helena. The scene quickly became bedlam—thousands of merrymakers thronged the downtown and spilled into the residential districts.

Hotels, boarding houses, and public buildings filled and overflowed. Helenans who had registered their accommodations with the Young Men's Capital Club at Sixth and Main were assigned visitors. Citizens offered their extra beds and pantries to perfect strangers, all in the spirit of victory. Cafes and restaurants cooked nonstop, days and nights, often giving away the meals.

Throughout Monday, the 13 regular passenger trains into Helena disgorged hundreds of celebrants. "Capital Specials" also arrived from across the state: one from Great Falls at noon; another from Missoula at 2:00 P.M.; a third from Livingston-Bozeman at 3:00; the Marysville special an hour later; the Butte charter at 5:00. From these trains poured additional hundreds of enthusiastic "friends" into Helena's streets and businesses. They joined crowds that seemed to follow the seven or eight marching bands around the town.

The 5:00 P.M. "Butte Special" carried Helena's darlings, W.A.

Clark and John M. Quinn, in addition to more than 500 supporters. The *Helena Independent* reported (November 13, 1894):

"The arrival of the special at the Montana Central depot was the occasion for one of the most thrilling scenes of the day. By 4:30 there was a delegation of over 1,000 to welcome Mr. Clark. Hundreds of men and women wore badges with the name and picture of 'the Great Friend of Helena' printed thereon, and cheers for Clark were in order long before the train arrived. The crowds surrounded the depot and even collected in large groups upon the bluffs overlooking the scene.

"Finally the train backed in, and then for a few moments pandemonium reigned. All stood on their toes and yelled, yelled as they never had yelled before, for W.A. Clark. He was caught as he stepped from the train, and strong arms carried him bodily to the festooned carriage that stood in waiting. John M. Quinn was put in beside Mr. Clark and ex-Governor Samuel T. Hauser and Judge William H. Hunt completed the party. While the crowd cheered, a cannon a block away boomed its welcome as fast as the gunners could reload."

Clark's triumphant procession from the depot to the Helena Hotel proved even more remarkable:

"All at once the horses were taken from Mr. Clark's carriage, someone attached a long rope, and in a moment 200 citizens had hold of the line. The shouting body then started up Fuller Avenue toward town, pulling the distinguished party in the carriage.

"When they turned onto Lawrence and up Main, the streets were black with cheering crowds. The guns boomed, the bands played, and amidst the general uproar could be heard the measured shouts of the white-hatted brigade as it pulled the carriage to the cry of 'CLARK—CLARK—W.—A.—CLARK.'

"Men, women, and children waved their hats as they cheered. The parade turned up Broadway and went around to Grand Street to the Helena Hotel. An immense crowd formed around the carriage. When Clark and Quinn finally were able to get into the hotel, the crowd followed."

Monday evening's parade was designed as the centerpiece of Helena's victory celebration. At 7:00 P.M., under a full moon, on the mild, slightly windy evening, parade organizers started the march at the County Courthouse. Moving first north to Eleventh Avenue, the march circled back on Rodney and dropped down into the Gulch on Bridge Street. After winding through the downtown, it climbed to the West Side and ran along Madison Avenue to Hauser, before retracing its path into the business district. Finally climbing Broadway to Warren, the procession turned north until it disbanded at the Auditorium (a handsome building then on the northwest corner of Seventh and Warren, just south of present-day Central School).

By Montana standards, Helena's victory parade was tremendous: more than 120 entries; 9 marching bands from across the state; dozens of four-horse floats; torch-carrying fraternal groups; drum-rattling ranks of Civil War veterans; mounted "Helena for Capital" organizers from all over Montana; a contingent of uniformed Post Office employees; a similar corps from the Helena Fire Department; members of the statewide Afro-American Capital Club.

The parade took more than an hour to pass any point along its route. Approximately 1,500 people comprised the column. Another cheering 15,000 watched it from sidewalks, from building windows, from house porches, from hillsides, from every available perch. The crowd remained raucous, blowing horns and igniting fireworks. The parade route was lit by hundreds of marchers' torches, as well as by all three bonfires on Mount Helena.

Some of the favorite horsedrawn floats depicted "the Helena Hog," "Miss Liberty," "the Helena High Five," and "Miss Helena and Her Court." The parade also included the hapless victims of election bets—pushing their victors in wheelbarrows, or marching in chicken suits, or carrying sandwich-boards proclaiming their transgressions. Noise generated by the throng remained deafening along every block of the route.

The parade ended at the bunting-bedecked Auditorium, already packed with boisterous, chanting celebrants. The milling overflow pushed on to the Opera House. Beginning at 9:00 P.M., speakers moved between the two buildings, haranguing the jubilant crowds until orators and celebrants alike lost their voices. Receptions followed in the Auditorium, in the capital-club offices, and in private homes around town. The Montana Club sponsored an exclusive gathering for the members of Helena's influential "Speakers Bureau."

Most of the merrymakers, however, spilled into the downtown district. Here the marching bands and thousands of revelers surged up and down the torchlit streets until well after midnight. Barkeeps poured free drinks and waitresses served free food. Fireworks exploded continuously, and the whole melee was lit by Mount Helena bonfire light. Helena has never celebrated on such a scale—before or since. W.A. Clark reportedly picked up a bar bill of $30,000 for the festivities.

A somewhat subdued hoard of revelers greeted Tuesday morning. The out-of-town celebrants boarded their "specials" and steamed away. Yet many visitors remained, and the bands played all afternoon on street corners along Main Street. Community leader Thomas Cruse hosted an open-house reception for thousands of Helena supporters at his home on Benton and Lawrence, from 2:00 P.M. until 11:00 that night. The *Independent* observed (November 14, 1894):

"There was no 'social supremacy' at Colonel Cruse's reception. Bankers, merchants, matrons, clerks, day laborers—all touched elbows within the hospitable mansion. A delicious lunch of salads and other delicacies was spread, and visitors washed it down with sparkling wine and delicious punch.

"It was a great reception and all the greater because there was no formality beyond the usual handshakes and greetings. The invitation was to all, and all were there! The Colonel's open house was perhaps the best symbol of Helena's true character—and of her victory over Anaconda, for all the people of Montana."

After a vicious, corrupt election campaign, Helena's supporters organized and executed a classy victory demonstration—one truly worthy of a community that had captured the permanent capital. Helena's success on November 6, 1894, assured "the Queen City" a solid economic future. And many of us live here today because of that remarkable election triumph.

"SLAMS OF LIFE": HELENA AND THE 1918 INFLUENZA EPIDEMIC

BY JON AXLINE

What is it like this Spanish Flu?
Ask me, brother, for I've been through.
It is by misery out of despair;
It pulls your teeth and curls your hair;
It thins your blood and brays your bones;
And fills your craw with moans and groans;
And sometimes, maybe, you'll get well,
Some call it flu—I call it hell!

J.P. McEnvoy, 1919

During the dark days of the first World War, the United States was assailed by the Central Powers overseas and a deadly strain of influenza virus at home. The disease, known as the Spanish flu, eventually took more American lives on the home front than did the war in Europe. Helena was not spared the ravages of the flu, for which there was no proven vaccine. Unfortunately, the city's residents were little prepared for the pestilence and it exacted a terrible toll on them.

The disease included all the loathsome symptoms that we've grown accustomed to during modern flu seasons. The malady included fever, nausea, a "feeling of weakness," depression and a "hard cough." Because the virus attacked the mucous lining of the air passages, it gave all the appearance of a severe head cold. The virus, however, also caused bronchitis, pneumonia and, occasionally, encephalitis. All the influenza-related deaths in Helena were caused by pneumonia.

The Red Cross found a simpler way of preventing the spread of the flu—they began production of gauze masks that were distributed by the local Odd Fellows chapter.

Spanish influenza first appeared on the East Coast in mid-September 1918. Although one Helena newspaper editor claimed the disease arrived in the United States via a German submarine off New York City, it was likely transported to this country by ships arriving from Spain. Within a few weeks of its appearance in the East, the virus arrived in northeast Montana where it took a heavy toll in Plentywood, Wolf Point and Poplar. The influenza reached Helena on October 9, when ten cases were reported to the City Health Officer, Dr. William Cogswell.

Because of the war in Europe, the state and city were experiencing a shortage of doctors. As the influenza gained a stranglehold on the community, the remaining doctors found themselves overwhelmed with new cases. Although the State Board of Health required that all cases of the disease be reported, the physicians found they were unable to file the necessary reports because of the sheer number of victims. While they reported a substantial number of new cases each day, at least three times that number of people actually had the sickness.

The influenza crept into Helena so slowly that State Board of Health Chief Ashburn Barbour saw no reason to take precautions against a general outbreak of the disease. Instead, he believed the virus posed no real danger to Helena because of the "absence of crowds and the abundance of sunshine" in the city. He recommended that the citizenry "go to bed, stay quiet, take a laxative, eat plenty of nourishing food, keep up [its] strength, nature is the cure." Nonetheless, Barbour suggested the city begin sprinkling the streets and that the streetcar companies improve the ventilation of their trolleys. The first flu-related death occurred on October 13, when "the popular young manager of the Interstate Lumber Company," Elbert Nider, succumbed to pneumonia.

Rumors about the extent of the disease in Helena caused the city officials to initiate an investigation. Because local doctors did not have time to fill out reports for each new case, the number of those afflicted in the city was rumored to be anywhere from "scores" to "hundreds." That there was some truth to the rumors is supported by the fact that Dr. Cogswell ordered the closure of all Helena schools, churches, theaters and the YMCA shortly after the investigation began. He also forbade public gatherings and directed the police to remove all tables and chairs from the local saloons. Within a week, the order was expanded to include the closure of the Shrine Auditorium, Carroll College, the public library, and all pool and card rooms. No political rallies were allowed and caterers were not allowed to accept any banquet orders.

On October 18, Western Union employees began wearing military-style gas masks to prevent the spread of the disease. The fashion was later adopted by workers at the Union Bank & Trust and the American National Bank. The telephone operators had a harder time of it, finding it difficult to ask "number please?" when wearing a gas mask. The Red Cross found a simpler way of preventing the spread of the disease—they began production of gauze masks, which were distributed by the local Odd Fellows chapter. On October 24, the city made it mandatory for cooks, waiters, bartenders, hairdressers and store clerks to wear the masks. The newspaper provided instructions on how to make and disinfect the masks. Although the number of influenza cases increased, the city relaxed the mask order somewhat after "numerous persons...complained that the constant wearing of the masks subjected them to severe headaches...eye strains and other inconveniences."

Because the State Board of Health was located in Helena, the city was fortunate to be one of the first recipients of a vaccine developed to prevent the flu. Consisting of a series of three shots, the untested Rosenow Anti-influenza Vaccine was given to 1,000 Helenans on November 9 and was hardily received. Two days later, armistice was signed in Europe and all hell broke loose in Helena as jubilant citizens ignored the ban on public gatherings to celebrate the end of the war. Although the sanctions were reimposed on November 12, the mood was grim in the city when Cogswell announced that there were 1,252 reported cases of the Spanish influenza in Helena between October 10 and November 12. About six percent of the city's population had contracted the disease. Of those, 72 city and county residents died as a result of complications of the disease. The number of influenza cases peaked on October 28 when 92 new cases of the pestilence were reported in the city.

The number of new cases of the flu in Helena abated after the middle of November as the disease ran its course. The sanctions imposed by Dr. Cogswell were lifted by early 1919. The Spanish influenza infected 26,607 Montanans before it subsided. Of those, 2,436 died; ironically, only 934 Montanans were killed in combat in Europe. The influenza plague was an unfortunate consequence of Montana and Helena entering the national mainstream.

The disease made no distinction between the urban and rural areas of the state and had a devastating effect on both. It is difficult to gauge the impact of the disease on Helena. The city was woefully unprepared for the pestilence, trusting in its isolation and "clean mountain air" to spare it from the flu's ravages. It definitely interrupted the city's routine and dulled Helena's participation in the war effort (although not the celebration of its end). Fortunately, we've had nearly eighty years to build up an immunity to annual influenza outbreaks that are just as deadly as the Spanish flu; now, however, we know what to expect and can take the necessary precautions. So, the next time you catch the flu, remember the 1918 epidemic and count yourself lucky that it's not as bad as it could be.

UFOs Sighted in Helena

BY JON AXLINE

No one would have believed in the last years of the nineteenth century that this world was being watched keenly and closely by intelligences greater than man's, yet as mortal as his own...Yet across the gulf of space, minds that are to our minds as ours are to the beasts that perish, intellects vast cool and unsympathetic regarded this earth with envious eyes and slowly and surely drew their plans against us.

H.G. Wells

October 1938 brought the first of three invasions of Helena from outer space. The first occurred as a result of a radio show broadcast from New York. The other two "invasions" were the product of the flying-saucer craze that gripped the United States after World War II. All three events reflected the fears many Americans felt because of the Nazis before World War II and again because of the communists during the first years of the Cold War.

Helenans who attended the Rio Theater's matinee double feature of the original *Dracula* and *Frankenstein* on October 30, 1938, were in for a treat at six o'clock on the local Columbia Broadcasting affiliate, KFBB out of Great Falls. That's when Orson Welles' "Mercury Theater on the Air" presented a radio dramatization of H.G. Wells' novel *The War of the Worlds*. For those "channel surfing" between NBC's Edgar Bergen and Charlie McCarthy show and CBS, the program gave all indications of being an actual invasion from the planet Mars with live remotes from the invader's beachhead in New Jersey and bulletins describing the death and destruction wreaked by the Martians. Believing the invasion real, thousands on the East Coast and in the Midwest actually fled the imagined Martian war machines within an hour after the broadcast began.

Although spared the frenzy gripping other parts of the country, Helena was not sheltered from the Martian invasion. The *Helena Independent* reported that it was "swamped with telephone calls from frightened local residents who thought sure the world was coming to a disastrous end at the hands of the monsters..." While most phone calls were from women, the newspaper related, not a few men "with voices of fear" also telephoned the *Independent* wanting to know if they should make for the nearest root cellar.

One Helena caller heard a report that a Martian, who had disembarked from a meteorite, was tearing up the railroad tracks when it was attacked by the National Guard. After a hard fought battle, she believed, the "strange visitor" had utterly destroyed the 7,000 man militia, leaving only 125 survivors. Other Helenans sat glued to their radios awaiting either the end of the program or, if more gullible, the end of their lives at the hands (or tentacles) of the Martians.

Twelve years later, on April 12, 1950, Helena was again visited by strangers from the sky. This time, however, they came to Rodney Street. A 59-year-old bookkeeper, Mrs. Ida Welch, reported that while walking to a nearby grocery store late in the afternoon, she spotted an object that looked like "two soup plates put together" flying above the intersection of Rodney and Sixth Avenue. Welch stated that the unidentified object was "bigger than a bomber" and so close to the ground that anyone "could have shot it down with a rifle." After passing Mrs. Welch, the device traveled swiftly toward the Helena Middle School before it was lost to view past old U.S. Highway 91.

Mrs. Welch reported the incident to the Civil Air Administration control tower at the airport. They claimed there were no regularly scheduled flights in the Helena area at that time and that the object did not show up on radar. Undaunted, Mrs. Welch told the newspaper that "Truman, nor nobody else, can tell me they don't exist—I saw this one."

Three months after Mrs. Welch's sighting, Helena was again visited by a strange object in the sky. This time, however, it was also reported in Great Falls, Whitehall and Spokane. Shortly after midnight on July 3, five Helena residents at four different locations reported a UFO that was described either as cigar-shaped, a flaming disc or wing-shaped. The object was first sighted just after midnight by a man parked at Canyon Ferry dam with his girlfriend. A bartender at the Mint Bar on North Main reported seeing the UFO at about the same time.

A Mrs. A.H. Tuttle and her daughter spotted the object while walking home from the late movie shortly after midnight on Park Street. Far from being terrified, Mrs. Tuttle reported that the wing-shaped mechanism "looked as though it was made of brass and generated its own light, but did not seem to be flaming.... It was beautiful."

The last observer described a "whirling disc" streaking eastward about 12:15 A.M. Sunday. The man, who was driving back to Helena from Elk Park, said the UFO left an orange and white trail behind it and was at an altitude of between eight and ten thousand feet. Eyewitnesses in Whitehall and Great Falls also reported seeing the UFO at approximately the same time.

Orson Welles' "War of the Worlds" proved to be the ultimate Halloween prank; it even hoodwinked people as far away as Helena, Montana. In the 1950s, however, many argued that flying saucers were also a prank being perpetrated on a credulous public by who knows what. So, keep in mind this October 31 that "grinning, glowing, globular invader of your living room is an inhabitant of the pumpkin patch and if your doorbell rings and there's nobody there, that was no Martian, it's Halloween."

It Still Happens at the Lewis & Clark County Fair

BY CHERE JIUSTO

Helena hosted the first territorial fair in September 1870. Sponsored by the Montana Agricultural, Mineral and Mechanical Association, the event took place on land leased from Madam Coady, proprietress of the Ten Mile House, on the outskirts of Helena.

Enterprising fair founders built three fair buildings in one month: Floral Hall, Mechanical Hall and Agricultural Hall. At the same time, a one-mile racetrack was constructed, described at the time as "the finest in the territories." A couple of decades later a trainload of "special dirt" was hauled in from Kentucky to upgrade that track, which remains today the only one-mile track in the Northwest.

In addition to horse racing, main attractions at the fair were agricultural exhibits, appearances by politicos of all stripes, and "a snug outdoor saloon where any and all who thirst can be accommodated."

As Montana grew up, the territorial fair became the Montana State Fair, so designated by Governor Joseph Toole in 1903.

Over the years, special events took place at the State Fair and history was made. In 1893, two bicycle riders departed from Helena's Fairgrounds, headed for the Chicago World's Fair.

LEWIS & CLARK

A Lewis & Clark County Fair exhibit early in the 20th century.

In 1909, President William Howard Taft made an appearance. And in 1913, pioneer pilot Katherine Stinson flew the first air-mail route in Montana—from the Fairgrounds to the Helena post office.

Drought, the homestead bust and widespread economic depression all took a toll on the state fair, however, and during the late 1910s and the 1920s participation and attendance declined. Failing crops and bank foreclosures caused many rural counties to drop away; most people simply couldn't afford to travel to Helena to attend. The last state fair was held in Helena in August of 1932.

During the years that followed, Helena's Fairgrounds stood idle and the buildings fell apart. Wind whistled through the grandstand carrying with it the fading echoes of hoofbeats at the trackside. For two decades, nothing stirred at the capital city Fairgrounds but an occasional dust devil.

Then in 1958 a group of determined fair lovers revived the dream of a local fair. A county-fair board was formed, fair buildings were rebuilt and in 1961 the first Last Chance Stampede Rodeo—a one-day affair—was held.

Finally in 1969, after a 37-year lull, the fair was reborn in Lewis and Clark County. In 1994, the Lewis and Clark County Fair marked its 25th anniversary, much to the credit of those who would not let our local fair die. Many long-time Helenans stand out among that group, especially Bill Carson, who is credited with having saved the fair and the Fairgrounds as well.

Today, the Lewis and Clark County Fair, along with the Last Chance Stampede, is one of Helena's best-loved summer events. From animals and home-made jams, to wild rides, corn-dogs, and the midway, to bronc riding, barrel racing and wild-cow milking, after more than a century, it all still happens at the fair. See you there!

LOST IN HELENA

BY DAVE WALTER

The story has gained credibility with each rolling decade. As told in Helena's cafes, sitting rooms, and barber shops, jovial President William Howard Taft visited in the fall of 1909—only to elude his Secret Service bodyguards and disappear for hours in the streets of Helena. Depending on the storyteller, the President was visiting old friends, or sitting in a saloon on South Main, or sampling the bawdy offerings of Clore Street.

The Taft tale, like any worthwhile yarn, holds just enough truth to remain alive. Yet the historical truth—the reality of the event—always proves more compelling than the fabrication. A look at "the rest of the story" is most illuminating.

Indeed, Republican President Taft visited "the Capital City" on Monday, September 27, 1909—less than one year after Montanans had given him their majority in the 1908 election. By reaching Helena, he completed about one-third of a truly ambitious 57-day railroad tour around the United States, snaking from Boston through the Midwest, to the West Coast, and back to Washington, D.C. The almost 14,000-mile tour comprised the longest excursion by a President-in-office to that time.

Before 1909 only President Theodore Roosevelt had visited Helena (May 27, 1903). Yet after Taft's stop, four other sitting presidents appeared here: Woodrow Wilson (September 11, 1919); Warren G. Harding (June 29, 1923); Harry Truman (May 12, 1950); George Bush (September 18, 1989). Regardless of the era, the appearance of a President-in-office generated enormous community enthusiasm and lifelong memories.

Such proved the case on September 27, 1909, when Taft's special train arrived from Butte and approached the Lewis and

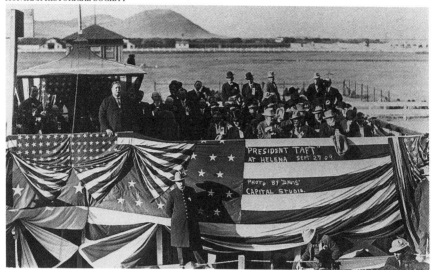

President Taft speaking at the Montana State Fair at the Fairgrounds on September 27, 1909.

Clark County Fairgrounds on a Great Northern Railway spur line. The President planned to attend the 7th Annual Montana State Fair on its opening day—declared "Taft Day" by Montana Governor Edwin L. Norris.

Helena's civic leaders had prepared thoroughly. With a population of fewer than 12,000, the capital expected at least another 5,000 visitors to descend on the town to see the President and to revel in "State Fair Week." The Helena Commercial Club (predecessor of the Chamber of Commerce) organized residents to take visitors into their homes once the hotels and boarding houses filled. The entire town sported flags and bunting, and store owners promised to close during Taft's four-hour stay so their employees could participate.

Helena's reception committee alone numbered more than 400 persons—including state officials, district judges, directors of the State Fair, members of the legislature, and delegates from all of Montana's 28 counties. Although Montana's entire Congressional contingent—Senators Thomas H. Carter and Joseph M. Dixon, and Representative Charles N. Pray—was Republican, Taft's visit rose above obvious partisanship to patriotism.

Organizers forecast the largest crowds in Helena since "the Queen City" had celebrated its state-capital victory in 1894. The late September weather was perfect: sunny, in the mid-70s, with light breezes. As many as 10,000 people were expected to crowd the Fairgrounds to hear Taft's first speech.

A motorcade then would trail into town to the recently constructed Federal Building (the current City-County Building on Park, at the west end of Sixth Avenue). Here the President would address Helena's school children. Finally the cavalcade would exit the business district via Helena Avenue to the Northern Pacific depot, where the President's special train awaited. An air of excitement and jubilation imbued the town on Monday.

Because of the assassination of President William McKinley only eight years earlier, security for Taft remained tight. Secret Service bodyguards not only accompanied the President, but also filtered through the town. Both the Northern Pacific and the Great Northern railroads provided special plainclothes agents who worked the crowds.

Helena Police Chief Jack Flannery also received assistance from the county sheriff's deputies, the U.S. Marshal's men, and Helena's own private N.P. Walters Detective Agency. Finally, Montana Militia squads and U.S. Army 6th Infantry troops from Fort Harrison served as the President's escorts and cordoned off the parade route.

This security proved fortuitous, for the excitement at the Fairgrounds that afternoon reached pandemonium (*Montana Daily Record,* September 27, 1909):

"All State Fair attendance records were broken. The grandstand could hold no more than a fourth of the visitors. They filled the betting ring, the bleachers, the grounds in front of the grandstand, the stretch extending for a quarter of a mile west, and the infield. Every nook where a foothold could be obtained was occupied. Around the speakers' stand so closely were the people packed that it was difficult to even breathe.

"As the President's party approached the speakers' platform, a cry of welcome burst from over 10,000 throats. It was a great billow of sound, rising higher and higher, and it rolled across to Scratch Gravel, and the mountains caught it and flung it back. They too welcomed the first man in the land.

"Again and again the crowd burst into applause. The Boston and Montana Band played 'Hail to the Chief' as it had never played it before, but the tones were drowned in the vocal reception accorded Taft."

Following a 12-minute speech—in which the President praised Montana women, complimented the state's agricultural production, and urged Americans to embrace greater individual achievement—fair managers ran the one-mile-dash "Cowboy Race" for the President. Fanny Sperry (Steele) next was scheduled to perform a "bronco-busting exhibition" for the President. But, because he had fallen behind schedule, security quickly assembled the motorcade for the trip into Helena.

A Pathfinder security car preceded by 600 feet the parade of 11 open automobiles. It carried several Secret Service agents, N.P. Walters, Chief of Police Flannery, the Northern Pacific's W.J. McFatridge, and two U.S. Marshals. Helena physician Ben C. Brooke owned and drove Car #1. It contained: the President; Captain A.W. Butt, Taft's aide-de-camp; Governor Norris; Senator Carter. The procession left the Fairgrounds with an escort of mounted officers from Fort Harrison. It approached the town through lines of cheering citizens along North Benton Avenue.

At the angled intersection of Madison Avenue and North Benton, a milling crowd waited. Here a second mounted escort joined the automobiles. The prescribed parade route would ascend Madison Avenue to Lawrence, then run down Lawrence to Park Avenue and the new Federal Building. Up Madison Avenue the security car led several lines of mounted soldiers, who swept the parade route. At the last minute, however, President Taft diverted the rest of the column.

Amid confused policemen, Car #1 led the remaining autos farther south on Benton Avenue, left onto a side road, and up Capitol Hill. At the top, amid construction machinery, work horses, and piles of building stone, Catholic Bishop John Patrick Carroll greeted the dignitaries.

Surrounded by frocked clergy, students from St. Aloysius Academy, and honorees scrambling from the touring cars, Senator Carter introduced the Bishop to the President. In short order the two married church and state by dedicating the corner-

President Taft at Helena, September 27, 1909, in front of Common Brothers Company Grocers, corner of Sixth Avenue and Park Avenue.

stone for St. Charles Hall—the initial building in Bishop Carroll's "Capitol Hill College."

In response to brief words by the Bishop, President Taft extemporized (*Helena Daily Independent,* September 28, 1909):

"Though not of your faith, I cannot help but appreciate the good work your church is doing in this country.... I feel honored in being asked to take part in this ceremony—the laying of the cornerstone of what is undoubtedly destined to be a great educational institution. And I wish you God speed in the completion of the institution."

The dignitaries then climbed back into their autos, reformed the cavalcade, and descended Capitol Hill. The column turned south on Benton Avenue and resumed the original parade route by taking Hauser Avenue up the hill to Madison. The short diversion most aggravated the puzzled security agents sitting in their Pathfinder in front of the Federal Building, and hundreds of squirming school children assembled by their teachers at the site.

"On the steps of the Federal Building hundreds of little boys, dressed in natty suits of black, were so arranged in a sitting posture to spell the word 'T-A-F-T.'

"Each child on the lawn was supplied with a flag, and, as the President's auto came to a stop, the flags were waved vigorously by the youthful hands" (*Montana Daily Record,* September 28, 1909).

President Taft's enthusiastic, inspiring speech to the children created a warm conclusion to his visit to Helena. Soon the motorcade wound down Main Street and Helena Avenue to the Northern Pacific depot. By 7:00 P.M. the President's special had pulled out of Helena, heading west for Mullan Pass, Garrison, and Spokane.

So what about the story that Taft was "lost in Helena for hours, doing who-knows-what?" That tale developed because some chagrined security agents spent an embarrassing half hour at the Federal Building trying to explain to a boisterous crowd of school children that the President was right behind them.

Senator Tom Carter, a staunch Catholic, must be credited with persuading fellow Republican Taft to change the itinerary. Carter had promised Bishop Carroll that he could deliver the President on the spur of the moment—and he could. President Taft never was lost in Helena; he just could not say "no" to an old friend and an influential political ally.

In the end, the reality of President Taft's quick visit to Helena proves more compelling than the fable it generated. "Capitol Hill College" became Mount St. Charles College, which became Carroll College in 1932. This renowned educational institution—which Taft endorsed in 1909—has developed into an integral part of the Helena community. In 1994 it served over 1,425 students. It also invested in the Helena economy practically all of its $16.7 million budget—$6 million in salaries alone.

Carroll's role in the Helena story is as entwined as that of the six presidents who have visited here. Not one of those chiefs-of-state ever was lost in Helena—not even the jovial President Taft.

HELENANS PLAYED A CRUCIAL ROLE IN EXPLORATION OF YELLOWSTONE

BY RICHARD B. ROEDER

On March 1, 1872, President U.S. Grant signed a bill establishing Yellowstone country "as a public park or pleasuring ground for the benefit and enjoyment of the people," thus creating the world's first national park. Probably few current residents of Helena are aware of the crucial role early Helenans played in the exploration of the Yellowstone and the creation of the park.

Until after the Civil War the area later included in the park was largely *terra incognita*. Early reports about unusual features of the park by trappers and prospectors did not produce the usual rush of people to a new El Dorado. The seemingly wild accounts by trappers and prospectors were discounted by a public that had grown accustomed to their tall tales. This and the lack of gold and paucity of furs and the area's difficulty of access made it one of the last sections of the West subject to recorded, scientific information.

Prior to the creation of the U.S. Geological Survey in 1879, the country depended upon the army for exploration. The first attempt at army reconnaissance of Yellowstone was led by Captain William F. Raynolds in 1859–60. As usual, Raynolds' group included a naturalist, artist and topographer. As a study of the unusual features of Yellowstone, Raynolds' expedition was a failure. His orders directed him to locate the headwaters of the Yellowstone River. Raynolds explored the Big Horn Basin and the Wind River Mountains. Despite the aid of mountain man Jim Bridger as guide, snow and difficulty of terrain forced Raynolds around the park areas. When Raynolds returned to civilization he faced the task of preparing his men for secession and civil war. His reports remained unpublished until well after the war.

In the meantime, Montanans, especially those from Helena, assumed the initiative in exploration. Because of its location and early population, Helena was a jumping off place for ventures into what would become the park. In a few years their efforts transformed the Yellowstone from an unknown region into a national park.

In 1869 a group of Helena men discussed the possibility of civilian exploration and indicated their willingness to participate in such a task. When it became clear that no military escort from Fort Ellis east of Bozeman was to be had, a fear of Indian attacks caused most of the group to discover that the pressures of personal business forbade their participation. By summer's end the intrepid Charles W. Cook, David E. Folsom, and William Peterson decided they would go it alone.

The three well-armed men left Helena on September 6 and returned October 11. The group explored the Grand Canyon of the Yellowstone River, Yellowstone Lake and thermal activity in what would later be known as Lower Geyser Basin. After their return Cook and Folsom regaled friends with details of what they had seen. Despite Folsom's statement that "language is inadequate to convey a just conception of this masterpiece of nature's handiwork," and encouraged by the response of their friends in Helena, Folsom and Cook collaborated on a written account of what they had seen.

The *New York Tribune* and *Scribner's Monthly* magazine rejected the article as too fanciful to risk publication. Finally the two found a willing publisher in the *Western Monthly Magazine*, a Chicago periodical, which published the article in July 1870, the first written authentic report on the upper Yellowstone.

In his retelling of the story, Folsom repeated a suggestion made earlier by Thomas Francis Meagher, that the spectacular sites ought to be reserved from entry under the Homestead Act and preserved for the public. This proposal, an improved map of the area and the account in the *Western Monthly Magazine* were the immediate results of the expedition.

Little is known of Peterson's subsequent life because he soon moved to Idaho, but Cook and Folsom remained and became important citizens in the state's later history. Both were important pioneers in the sheep industry in Meagher County where both established ranches. Folsom, originally from New Hampshire, filled several county offices and was a member of the Capitol Commission to oversee construction of the State Capitol, a member of the state legislature, and an unsuccessful Republican candidate for governor in 1900. Cook, who hailed from Maine, was a successful banker as well as a sheep man.

Despite the skepticism of outsiders, the Cook-Folsom *Western Monthly* article and conversations with their friends revived interest among Helenans in a follow-up expedition. A small number of Helenans agreed to participate in an expedition if they could secure a military escort. Upon receiving assurances from the army that an escort would be available, a group led by Henry Dana Washburn left Helena August 17, 1870, for Fort Ellis several miles east of Bozeman. There the Helenans joined up with their escort. The expedition that left Fort Ellis consisted of nineteen men, including two black cooks, five soldiers under the command of Lieutenant Gustavus C. Doane, and eleven men from Helena.

Most of the Helena contingent included men of proven accomplishment who knew Cook and Folsom, and who already had, or would have, important careers in Montana. Washburn was a Civil War general and a two-term congressman from Indiana. Samuel T. Hauser, the most energetic organizer of the expedition, was a banker and investor in mining properties. As an entrepreneur of business interests, Hauser would be one of the most significant individuals in Montana's economic development. Cornelius Hedges was the founder of Montana's education system, a lawyer, journalist, and important Mason. Truman C. Everts was Assessor of Internal Revenue for Montana. Nathaniel P. Langford was Collector of Internal Revenue for Montana and Bank Examiner for the Territory, and would later be the first superintendent of Yellowstone National Park.

For the first leg of their journey, the Washburn-Doane Expe-

C.W. Cook.

dition, as it came to be called, followed the Cook-Folsom route. The group then struck out on its own to explore the eastern shore of Yellowstone Lake and most of the western shore. The group also explored the Upper Geyser Basin before picking up the headwaters of the Madison River for the return home.

By September 27, all the civilians had returned to Helena except for Truman C. Everts who, on September 9, had strayed from the main group and become lost. Repeated efforts by members of the expedition to find Everts proved fruitless.

Celebration of the group's return was dampened by the loss of Everts. Most of the Helena men feared that he had perished, and efforts at further search were abandoned until October 6 when some Helena citizens put up a reward of $600 to anyone who found Everts. In the meantime, Everts, having gradually lost all his equipment, including a magnifying glass that he used to start fires, subsisted on thistle roots. Two trappers, whose interest was stirred by the promised reward, went into

D.E. Folsom.

the Yellowstone country in search of Everts. On October 16 they found him, emaciated and near death.

The return of Everts was cause for celebration, but more importantly, his adventures gave a wide notoriety to the Washburn-Doane Expedition. The *Helena Herald* carried the story of Everts' travails and discovery. The *Herald's* reports were followed by Everts' own account, which he titled, "Thirty-seven Days of Peril." It appeared in the November 1871 issue of *Scribner's Monthly* and was a national sensation.

Others, especially Langford and Hedges, wrote articles describing their experiences and the magnificent creations of nature they had seen that heretofore seemed impossible to believe. In addition, Doane wrote an official military report, the first official account of what was to become Yellowstone National Park.

Given the size of the Washburn-Doane Expedition and the reputations of those who participated, the veracity of the various accounts could no longer be regarded as the tall tales of trappers and prospectors. The Washburn-Doane Expedition and the publicity it received inspired a third expedition, a scientific one that led directly to the creation of Yellowstone National Park. Even before this third expedition, a few Helena people had expressed the idea that the grandeur of the area ought to be reserved for public, rather than private, use. Finally, Folsom accurately predicted the later conflict between preservation and use. Of Yellowstone Lake he wrote, "We felt glad to have looked upon it before its primeval solitude would be broken by the crowds of pleasure seekers which at no distant day will throng its shores."

Historians cannot always supply clear, unambiguous answers to questions that are asked of them. A good case in point: to whom do we assign credit for the creation of Yellowstone National Park? This is a difficult question, partly because archival records are not the best, but most of the difficulty arises from the fact that there were several rival contemporary claimants, some of whom were self-proclaimed while others were recognized by their fellow citizens as park creators. Currently, a privately published circular used in the park credits Nathaniel Langford, who would be the park's first superintendent, with galvanizing people into the formation of the 1870 Washburn-Doane Expedition. The same publication asserts that members of this group, upon their return to civilization, organized a campaign to save the wonders of Yellowstone from private control and commercial exploitation. This is only partly true and needs to be carefully qualified.

Stories from the Washburn-Doane Expedition were early expressions of the need to protect Yellowstone from private entry under federal land law, but it was a third expedition—which the Washburn-Doane inspired—a scientific one, that was crucial to the creation of the park. This third expedition was led by Ferdinand Vanderveer Hayden, professor of geology at the University of Pennsylvania and a summertime federal geologist.

Following the return of the Washburn-Doane Expedition, the idea of establishment of a park was expressed by several members of the expedition, especially in columns in the *Helena Herald* by Cornelius Hedges and Nathaniel Langford. Langford also supported the park idea in several important speeches back East in New York City and Washington, D.C. Hayden's interest was aroused by Langford's writings and especially his speeches. He had also read Doane's official military report on the Yellowstone. As a government employee, Hayden was supposed to have spent the summer of 1871 on a natural history survey of parts of Wyoming and Nebraska, but intrigued by reports emanating from Helena, he secured permission to examine the Yellowstone country instead.

Meanwhile, among some Helena supporters of the park idea there was a growing fear that the wonders of nature would be privately exploited as squatters began to stake out claims at some of the most attractive sites. Park supporters responded by urging that the entire area be removed from the homestead laws as a means of preservation for eventual use by the general public. These efforts were significantly aided by Hayden's expedition of 1871. Upon his return from the field, Hayden devoted much of his time and influence in support and passage of the bill creating Yellowstone Park.

Hayden was a promoter as well as a scientist. He was very effective in working with congressmen to secure funds to support his scientific efforts. His fieldwork as a geologist would meld within a few years with that of other government scientists into the U.S. Geological Survey. His study was a typical scientific venture of that day and was the most far-reaching reconnaissance of the Upper Yellowstone. His group was large. It required twenty packers, hunters and laborers to keep the operation going and included metallurgists, entomologists, topographers, geologists and other naturalists. Hayden also included two novice frontiersmen, Thomas Moran and William Jackson. It was customary for scientific ventures to include artists to record flora, fauna and scenery. Moran was a landscape painter, and Jackson was an early practitioner of the relatively new technology of outdoor photography. Both were destined to achieve lasting national fame in their own rights. Congress later paid Moran $10,000 for his painting of the

F.V. Hayden.

grand canyon of the Yellowstone, and Jackson's photos came to be synonymous with Western scenes.

After Hayden's return to Washington, the bill creating the park passed with amazing speed. Introduction of the bill on December 18, 1871, was followed by passage on March 1, 1872. Montana's territorial delegate, William Clagett, who also authored the mining law of 1872 that has been the subject of much present-day discussion, claimed to have authored the bill and seen to its passage. He probably tried to claim too much. The condition of Montana's territorial archives and those of the House of Representatives do not enable historians to corroborate Clagett's claim. Hayden later claimed major honors for passage of the bill. Clearly, Hayden's work had confirmed information on the

W.H. Jackson.

Yellowstone, and he exercised his considerable influence with congressmen to push for passage of the bill. He used Jackson photos and hundreds of Moran sketches to educate congressmen as to the unusual qualities of the park area. When it came time to set the boundaries of the park, Congress relied heavily on Hayden. But, like Clagett, he may have claimed too much. By the time Hayden became involved, Eastern senators and congressmen had already begun to show an interest in the park idea.

To whom, then, do we assign credit for the creation of the park, the first national park in the world and one that would serve as a model for subsequent parks in the United States and elsewhere in the world? Langford gave credit to Cornelius Hedges for originating the park idea during a campfire discussion on September 19, 1870, when both were members of the Washburn-Doane Expedition. Hedges did not emphatically deny the truth of the story, and in later years he claimed that it was true. But others in Helena had come to the same conclusion, and he was not the only proponent of the idea. There is enough credit to bestow upon a considerable number of people, but the contributions of Helenans, especially Langford and Hedges, cannot be questioned.

A circumstance that united supporters of a public park was the condition of the American side of Niagara Falls. This was in private hands, and its exploitation had acquired for it an international reputation for the trashy and unappealing appearance that detracted from the pleasurable viewing of one of the world's great natural phenomena.

The park idea cannot be attributed to a single individual such as Langford claimed for Hedges. Nevertheless, the city of Helena deserves to be recognized as its cradle. Those involved in establishing the idea and passage of a bill to implement it did not have a clear vision of what the park would be. This is hardly surprising since they were groping for a concept of an unprecedented institution. Supporters of the park, however, were united by a common belief that the wonders of nature should be kept under public control for the future enjoyment of the country's general citizenry and that turning the park over to private hands would, inevitably, lead to its desecration.

Jon Axline, a Montana native, can trace his roots in Helena, through the Adami Family, back to 1872. As a Cultural Resource Specialist/Historian for the Montana Department of Transportation, he has had the opportunity to visit many of the places, famous, infamous and less well known, where Montana's history was made. Jon's articles in this volume reflect his interest in early transportation systems and events.

Ellen Baumler, a Kansas native, taught for ten years in Tucson, Arizona, before moving to Helena in 1988. With a Ph.D. in medieval studies and three summers of co-directing a field school in Italy, she now takes delight in the accessibility and relevance of Helena's history. Ellen coordinates Montana's National Register of Historic Places sign program at the State Historic Preservation Office.

Chere Jiusto came to Helena from upstate New York in 1976. A historian for the Historic Preservation Office of the Montana Historical Society, she directed the study of Helena's oldest historic districts. She is also a ceramic artist and a former resident of the Archie Bray Foundation.

Leanne Kurtz is a Helena native and a fourth-generation Montanan with roots in Pony, Montana. She studied history at Montana State University and journalism at the University of Montana (although she still considers herself a Bobcat at heart). Leanne is currently the Cultural Records Manager at the State Historic Preservation Office.

Harriett C. Meloy came to Helena in the early 1930s. She is active in many local and state organizations. She was on the staff of the Montana Historical Society library from 1957 to 1977. She also served on the original board of the Lewis and Clark County Historical Society.

Richard B. Roeder is a noted historian and Professor Emeritus at Montana State University. He was twice honored as the recipient of the Montana Award in the Humanities (1984 and 1988). With many publications to his credit, Rich is probably best known as the co-author of the definitive history of the state, *Montana: A History of Two Centuries.*

Dave Walter is a Montana historian, researcher, writer, editor, and teacher. Since 1979 he has worked at the Montana Historical Society in Helena, where he currently serves as the Society's Research Historian. Dave is the author of three books and scores of articles on the history of Montana and the West.